MCGRAW-HILL

Microsoft® **Windows** *98*

Timothy J. O'Leary

Arizona State University

Linda I. O'Leary

**Irwin
McGraw-Hill**

Boston   Burr Ridge, IL   Dubuque, IA   Madison, WI   New York   San Francisco   St. Louis
Bangkok   Bogotá   Caracas   Lisbon   London   Madrid
Mexico City   Milan   New Delhi   Seoul   Singapore   Sydney   Taipei   Toronto

Irwin/McGraw-Hill

A Division of The **McGraw·Hill** *Companies*

Microsoft® Windows 98

1 2 3 4 5 6 7 8 9 0 BAN BAN 9 0 0 9 8 7-9

ISBN 0-07-092041-9

Sponsoring Editor: Rhonda Sands
Developmental Editor: Kyle Thomes
Marketing Manager: Jodi McPherson
Production Supervisor: Melonie Salvati
Designer: Lorna Lo
Project Manager: Beth Cigler
Compositor: GTS Graphics
Typeface: 10/13 ITC Clearface
Printer: Banta

Library of Congress Cataloging-in-Publication Data
O'Leary, Timothy J., 1947-
    Microsoft Windows 98 / Timothy J. O'Leary. Linda I. O'Leary.
        p.   cm.
    Includes index.
    ISBN 0-07-092041-9
    1. Microsoft Windows (Computer file)   2. Operating systems
(Computers)   I. O'Leary, Linda I.   II. Title.
QA76.76.063045   1999
005.4'469—dc21   98-33571

http://www.mhhe.com

Contents

WNiv

Introduction to the Labs

Each lab module in the *McGraw-Hill Microcomputing* series consists of a sequence of labs that each require about one hour to complete. They are designed to provide you with practical skills in using the following kinds of software, which are the most widely used in business and industry:

- Windows 98
- Word processor
- Spreadsheet
- Database
- Graphics presentation
- Web browser

The labs describe not only the most important commands and concepts, but also explain why and under what circumstances you will use them. By presenting an ongoing case study based on input from actual business managers, we show how such software is used in a real business setting.

Organization of the Lab Modules

The Lab Modules Are Organized in the Following Categories: Overview, Labs, Case Project, Glossary of Key Terms, Command Summary, and Index.

Overview The overview, which appears at the beginning of each module, describes (1) what the program can do for you, (2) what the program is, (3) the generic terms that this and all similar programs use (for example, all word processing programs, regardless of brand name), and (4) the case study to be presented in the module for that program. The overview also includes a Before You Begin section, which presents information for both students and instructors about hardware and software settings and other items of importance to be considered before beginning the labs.

Labs The labs consist of both concept coverage and detailed, step-by-step directions for completing the problem presented in the case. The concepts appear in folder-like boxes preceding the step-by-step directions on how to apply the concept. Your progress through the labs is reinforced by the use of carefully placed figures that represent how your screen should appear after you complete a procedure. As you progress through the labs, the number of screen displays decreases and directions become less specific. This feature allows you to think about what you have learned, avoids simple rote learning, and reinforces earlier concepts and commands, helping you to gain confidence.

In case there is not enough lab time to complete the entire lab, the labs are often divided into two parts. When needed, instructions about how to end Part 1 and begin Part 2 appear at the end of Part 1.

Case Project Many lab modules include a complex project that allows you to apply and integrate the concepts you have learned throughout the labs.

Glossary of Key Terms The glossary, which appears at the end of each lab module, defines all the key terms that appear in bold in the overview and throughout the labs.

Command Summary Each lab module includes a quick-reference source for selected commands. The commands are listed in the order in which they appear in the application's menu.

Index Each lab module contains an index for quick reference to specific items within that module.

Organization of the Labs

The Labs Consist of the Following Parts: Competencies, Concept Overview, Case Study, Lab Review, Hands-On Practice Exercises, and Concept Summary.

Competencies The competencies list appears at the beginning of each lab. It lists the major concepts and features that you will have mastered upon completion of that particular lab.

Concept Overview Throughout the labs, the major concepts appear in folder-like boxes. The concept overview at the beginning of each lab provides a brief introduction to those concepts. They are in numbered order as presented in the lab.

Case Study The ongoing case study shows how to solve real-world business problems using the application covered by that particular module. The ongoing case study was written with the help of real-world experience contributed by industry managers. The specific case study used in each lab module is explained in the overview section for the module. You will follow the instructions in the labs to solve the case problems.

Lab Review The Lab Review includes a summary of terms and commands, as well as a variety of exercises designed to reinforce concepts and procedures presented in the lab. The review exercises do not require the use of a computer. The Lab Review consists of the following elements:

- *Key Terms* Terms that are defined in the labs appear in **boldface** type. They are also listed at the end of each lab in alphabetical order. The number of the page on which the term is introduced follows the term.

- *Command Summary* All commands that are used in the lab and the actions they perform are listed at the end of each lab in the order in which they appear on menus. The Command Summary also includes keyboard and toolbar shortcuts.

- *Matching, Fill-In, and Discussion Questions* A variety of different types of problems is presented. Matching problems emphasize both concepts and procedures through the use of traditional matching and identification exercises and action/result-type matching exercises. The fill-in questions are designed to reinforce concepts and key terms presented in the lab. Discussion questions encourage students to apply and expand upon what they have learned and reinforce concepts. Some discussion questions require that students use the World Wide Web to research a topic. These questions are identified with the On the Web icon shown in the margin.

Hands-On Practice Exercises The hands-on exercises following the Lab Review require the use of a computer to complete. This section is divided into two areas: Step by Step and On Your Own. The Step by Step exercises lead you through the steps needed to complete the problem. The On Your Own exercises provide limited directions. Each hands-on exercise is marked with stars that indicate the difficulty level of the problem. The star rating system is: *Easy, **Moderate, ***Difficult. Each section includes problems having a variety of difficulty levels.

Concept Summary The final item that appears at the end of each lab is the Concept Summary. This two-page spread presents a visual summary of the concepts presented in the lab.

Procedural Conventions

Commands and Directions Are Expressed Through Certain Standard Conventions.

We have followed certain conventions in the labs for indicating keys, key combinations, commands, command sequences, and other directions.

Keys Computer keys are expressed in abbreviated form, as follows:

Computer Keys	Display in Text
Alt (Alternate)	Alt
Backspace	Backspace
Caps Lock (Capital Lock)	Caps Lock
Ctrl (Control)	Ctrl
Del (Delete)	Delete
End	End
Esc (Escape)	Esc
(Enter/Return)	Enter
Home	Home
Ins (Insert)	Insert
Num Lock (Number Lock)	Num Lock
PgDn (Page Down)	Page Down
PgUp (Page Up)	Page Up
Print Screen	Print Screen
Scroll Lock	Scroll Lock
Shift	Shift
Tab	Tab

Function Keys

F1 through F12	F1 through F12

Cursor Movement

[↑] (Up)	↑
[↓] (Down)	↓
[←] (Left)	←
[→] (Right)	→

Key Combinations Many programs require that you use a combination of keys for a particular command (for example, the pair of keys Ctrl and F4). You should press them in the order in which they appear, from left to right, holding down the first key while pressing the second. In the labs, commands that are used in this manner are separated by a plus sign, for example, Ctrl + F4.

Directions The principal directions in the labs are "Press," "Move to," "Type," "Choose," "Select," and "Click." These steps are preceded with a bullet [■] and are in blue type.

■ *Press* This means you should strike a key. Usually a key will follow the direction. For example:

   ■ Press [Delete].

■ *Move to* This means you should move the insertion point or highlight to the location indicated. For example, the direction to move to cell A5 would appear as:

   ■ Move to A5.

■ *Type* This means you should type or key in certain letters or numbers, just as you would on a typewriter keyboard. Whatever is to be typed will appear in bright blue type. For example:

   ■ Type **January.**

■ *Choose and Select* A sequence of selections from a menu or dialog box is often required to complete a command. The selections are made using the mouse or keyboard. The command sequences will follow the word "Choose." If a letter of a command appears with an underline and in **boldface,** you can choose that command by typing the letter.

   "Select" is used to indicate selecting or marking an item from a list of available options. "Select" does not begin an action as "Choose" does. Selecting may be part of a command sequence and will usually appear when procedures are initially introduced. In the beginning these commands are introduced separately. For example:

   ■ Choose **F**ile.
   ■ Select **O**pen.
   ■ Select MEMBERS.DOC.

   Later, as you become more familiar with the program, the commands are combined on a single line. Each menu command selection may be separated by a /. For example,

   ■ Choose **F**ile/**O**pen/MEMBERS.DOC.

■ *Click* Commands that can be initiated using a button and the mouse appear following the word "Click." For example:

   ■ Click [💾] Save.
   ■ Click [OK].

Marginal Notes Throughout the labs notes appear in the margins. These notes may be reminders of how to perform a procedure, clarifications or alternate methods, or brief side notes that expand upon a concept. The marginal notes symbols have different meanings as illustrated below:

A standard informational note:

The menu equivalent is Format/Font/ Bold and the keyboard shortcut is $\boxed{Ctrl}$ + B.

An informational note for a mouse procedure:

"Double-click" means to click the left mouse button twice in rapid succession without moving the mouse.

An informational note for a keyboard procedure:

$\boxed{Tab}$ will make the next area active and $\boxed{Shift}$ + $\boxed{Tab}$ will make the previous area active.

A note that refers the reader back to information presented earlier:

Refer to Concept 7, Moving and Sizing windows for directions on how to move a window.

A warning note:

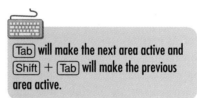

To avoid damaging files, always shut down Windows before you turn off your computer.

General System Requirements

To Complete the Labs, the Following Hardware and Software Are Needed:

- An IBM or IBM-compatible computer system with a hard disk and one or two floppy disk drives. The amount of RAM memory your computer must have varies with the application software program you will be using. If you are using a networked system, your instructor will provide additional instructions as needed.

- A mouse. Mouse use is assumed, although keyboard directions are provided as marginal notes.

- A printer.

- Windows 98 and the application software programs selected by your instructor and installed on your computer.

- Student data disk containing the files needed to perform the labs and to complete the hands-on practice exercises; these files are supplied by your instructor. They are also available from our Web page at http://www.mhhe.com/cit/concepts/oleary.

   Special Assumptions Any special directions or hardware and software assumptions that have been made in the preparation of these lab modules are described at the end of the overview for that particular software application module under the heading "Before You Begin."

Supplements

Each Lab Module Is Accompanied by the Following Supplements:

- *Teaching Materials* The Instructor's Manual provides lecture notes and guidelines for the instructor on the concepts and procedures presented in each lab. It also includes the answers to all lab review problems and hands-on practice exercises, as well as for the case project. In addition, a copy of the test bank questions and the test answer key is supplied.

- *Computerized Test Bank* A minimum of 40 true/false and multiple choice-type questions is supplied for each lab. With MicroTest III Computerized Test Bank, instructors can network a test in the lab, give students a test on disk, and prepare traditional pencil-and-paper tests. It also allows full editing of individual items.

■ *Instructor CD* The files that are required to complete the labs' hands-on practice exercises are provided on the data disk that is supplied with the teaching materials. They are also available from our Web page at http://www.mhhe.com/cit/concepts/oleary. Answers to all lab exercises are also included. The *PowerPoint Presentation* on the Instructor CD is a slide presentation including illustrations, screen shots, and lecture materials corresponding to the text.

Windows 98 Overview

Software is the set of instructions that directs the computer to process information. These instructions are also called programs. Without software, the computer cannot work. A commonly used analogy is that the computer hardware is the engine, while the software is the fuel that allows the engine to operate. Without software the hardware would be useless. There are two types of software: system software and application software.

System Software

System software consists of four kinds of programs designed to handle the physical complexities of how computer hardware works.

- The bootstrap loader is a program that is stored permanently in the computer's electronic circuitry. When you turn on your computer, the bootstrap loader obtains the operating system from your hard disk (or floppy disk) and loads it into memory. This is commonly called booting the system.

- The diagnostic routines are also programs stored in the computer's electronic circuitry. They start up when you turn on the machine. They test the primary storage, the central processing unit (CPU), and other parts of the system. Their purpose is to make sure the computer is running properly. On some computers, the screen may say "Testing RAM" (a form of computer memory) while these routines are running.

- The basic input-output system consists of service programs stored in primary storage. These programs enable the computer to interpret keyboard characters and transmit characters to the monitor or to a floppy disk

- The operating system provides the interface between the user and the computer and oversees the processing of the application programs and all input and output of the system. Without the operating system, you could not use the application software programs provided with this book. The operating system controls computer system resources and coordinates the flow of data to and from the microprocessor, and to and from input and output devices such as the keyboard and the monitor.

The operating system is usually provided by the computer manufacturer. The various types of computers require different types of operating systems in order to operate. Some of the most popular are Macintosh operating system, OS/2, Windows 95 and 98, and Unix.

Application Software

Application software is designed for specific uses or "applications," such as word processing, graphics, or spreadsheet analysis. Application software can be custom written but is usually purchased ready-made.

Normally, to use an application program, you load the program into the computer's memory; execute (run) the program; and then create, edit, or update a file. When you finish you need to save the work you have done on a disk. If you do not save your work and you turn off the computer, it is erased from memory and everything you have done will be lost.

The operating system acts as a communications link between the hardware and the application program. It is responsible for loading the application software into memory and then starting the program. It also retrieves data files and saves them to disk when directed. When you finish using the application software, you are returned to the operating system.

Microsoft Windows

The most widely used operating system for personal computers is Microsoft Windows. Windows 98 is the newest version of the Windows operating system. Like earlier versions, it has a graphical user interface (GUI, pronounced "gooey"). This kind of interface displays graphical objects called icons, which represent the items you use. The icons when selected activate the item.

All programs that use the Windows operating system have a common user interface that makes it easy to learn and use different programs that run under Windows. A common user interface means that programs have common features, such as the same menu commands. For example, you will find the command to open a file is the same in all Windows 95 applications.

The Windows operating system gets its name from its use of rectangular boxes, called windows, that are used to display information and other programs. Multiple windows can be open at the same time, making it easy to move from one task to another. This is how people work. More than likely you have several projects you are working on during the day, and need to be able to switch easily from one to the other.

Windows 98 Terminology

application software: Software programs that are designed to help you accomplish a specific task, such as creating a letter or an income statement.

graphical user interface (GUI): A design that uses graphical objects called icons, which represent the items you can select to activate the feature.

icon: A graphical object that when selected activates a feature.

operating system: The system software that provides the interface between the computer and the user.

program: A set of instructions that directs the computer to process information. Also called software.

software: A set of instructions that directs the computer to process information. Also called a program.

system software: A variety of programs that coordinate the operation of the various hardware components of the computer and oversee the processing of the application programs and all input and output of the system.

window: A rectangular box that is used to display information and other programs.

Before You Begin

To the Student:

The following assumptions have been made:

- The Windows 98 operation system has been properly installed on the hard disk of your computer system.

To the Instructor:

The following assumptions about the setup of the Windows 98 program have been made:

- Web style view is on by default (Start/Settings/Active Desktop/View as Web Page).

- The Active Desktop feature is off (Start/Settings/Active Desktop/Customize my Desktop/View my Active Desktop as a Web page).

- The following features in the My Computer window and Exploring window are on: Standard Buttons toolbar with text labels, Address Bar, status bar, Large Icon view. The window view is as a Web page.

- The All Folders Explorer Bar is displayed in the Exploring window.

- Data files are available for students to copy from a subfolder named Windows 98 in the Student Data Files folder.

- The Windows 98 supplemental applications WordPad, Calculator, Media Player, and Clipboard Viewer have been installed. To install these, use Add/Remove Programs from the Control Panel.

Windows 98 Basic Skills

COMPETENCIES

After completing this lab, you will know how to:

1. Start a computer and load Windows 98.
2. Use a mouse.
3. Use menus.
4. Start and use the Help program.
5. Use a scroll bar.
6. Use text boxes and dialog boxes.
7. Open multiple windows.
8. Move, size, and arrange windows.
9. Check disk properties and contents.
10. Change icon views.
11. Arrange icons.
12. Shut down Windows 98.

This lab introduces you to many of the basic skills that are needed to use a personal computer. You will develop these skills while learning about the Windows 98 operating system. This includes learning how to use a mouse, work with windows, use menus and dialog boxes, use the Help system, and explore the contents of your computer.

Learning to use these features is the foundation upon which your computer skills will continue to grow as you apply and expand your knowledge. This is because the features and concepts that are presented are common to all programs that use the Windows operating system.

Concept Overview

The following concepts will be introduced in this lab:

1. **Operating System**   An operating system is a collection of programs that helps the computer manage its resources and that acts as the interface between the user and the computer.

2. **Desktop**   The desktop is the opening screen for Windows 98 and is the place where you begin your work using the computer.

3. **Menu**   A menu is one of many methods used to tell a program what you want it to do. When opened a menu displays a list of commands.

4. **Window**   A window is a rectangular section of the screen that is used to display information and other programs.

5. **Dialog Box**   A dialog box is how Windows programs provide and request information from you in order to complete a task.

6. **File**   The information a computer uses is stored electronically as a variety of different files on a disk.

7. **Folder**   A folder is a named area on a disk that is used to store related subfolders and files.

8. **Moving and Sizing Windows**   Moving and sizing windows allows you to conveniently view information on your desktop.

9. **Arranging Windows**   There are two ways to arrange windows on the desktop, cascade and tile.

10. **Undo**   The Undo feature allows you to reverse your last action or command.

11. **Properties**   Properties are the settings and attributes associated with an object on the screen, such as an icon.

Part 1

Starting Windows 98

The primary purpose of a computer is to run application software designed to help you accomplish a task. However, in order to run application software, all computers must first load an operating system that controls the overall activity of the computer.

Refer to the Overview for a discussion of software.

Concept 1: Operating System

An **operating system** is a collection of programs that helps the computer manage its resources and that acts as the interface between the user and the computer. The three main functions of an operating system are to control hardware, manage information, and run application software. Hardware control consists of coordinating the different parts of the computer system so that all parts work together. This includes coordinating the flow of data to and from the system unit and to and from input and output devices like the keyboard and the display screen. Information management consists of controlling computer system resources, and includes providing the means to manage and store information on the computer. Running application software consists of loading programs designed for specific uses, such as word processing, graphics, and spreadsheet analysis.

The operating system you will learn about in this lab is Microsoft Windows 98, the newest version of the Windows operating system. Several features of this operating system that you will learn about and use in these labs are described below.

- Graphical user interface that uses pictures to represent familiar objects.

- Web style view that makes the operating system look and act much like a Web browser program.

- Multitasking capability that allows you to efficiently run multiple applications at the same time.

- Common user interface that makes it easier and faster to learn other applications.

The first thing you need to do is to turn on the computer. When you turn it on, the operating system loads automatically. This process is called a **cold start.** Flipping the power switch located on the back or right side of your computer or pushing the button on the front of your computer turns on most computers. You may also need to turn on the monitor and adjust the color and brightness. The button to turn it on and the dials to adjust it are generally located on the front of the monitor.

Your computer is on if you can hear the fan running and, on many machines, lights are lit on the front. If your computer is not on already, follow the instructions below to turn it on and load Windows 98.

- Turn on the power switch.

- If necessary, turn your monitor on and adjust the contrast and brightness.

- If you are on a network, you may be asked to enter your User Name and Password. Type the required information in the boxes, pressing [←Enter] after each.

Do not have any disks in the drives when you start the computer.

You can also press [Tab] to move to the next box.

The system and hardware checks are performed, and the Windows 98 program is loaded into the main memory of your computer. After a few moments, the Windows 98 logo is displayed. This screen is quickly followed by the Windows 98 screen and a Welcome to Windows 98 box as shown in Figure 1-1.

Welcome box provides
introductory information
about Windows 98

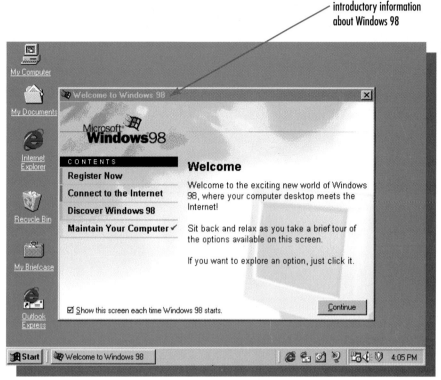

FIGURE 1-1

If the Welcome box is not displayed, this feature has been turned off. If this is the case, skip to the following section, "Exploring the Desktop."

The Welcome box includes several options that when selected allow you to register with Microsoft and access information about different features, such as an overview to Windows 98 and a discussion of how to maintain your computer. To close the box,

■   Press [Alt]+[F4] (If you know how to use a mouse, you can click [X] in the upper right corner of the box).

The Welcome box is closed, and your screen should be similar to Figure 1-2.

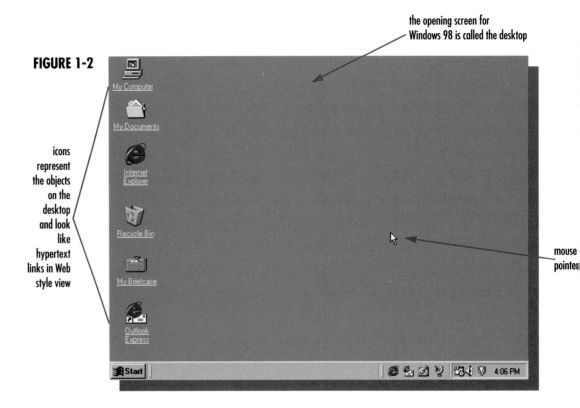

the opening screen for
Windows 98 is called the desktop

FIGURE 1-2

icons
represent
the objects
on the
desktop
and look
like
hypertext
links in Web
style view

mouse
pointer

Exploring the Desktop

Your screen displays the Windows desktop, from which you access the tools you need to use the computer.

Concept 2: Desktop

The **desktop** is the opening screen for Windows 98 and is the place where you begin your work using the computer. It is called a desktop because it provides quick access to the tools you need to complete your work using the computer. Small pictures, called **icons,** represent the objects on the desktop. Like your own desk at home or work, you can add and remove objects from the desktop, rearrange them, or get rid of them by throwing them into the "trash." You can also open some objects, much like a drawer in your desk, to access other tools or materials you have stored in it. You can then place these items on the desktop, or take items off the desktop and place them in the "drawer."

Just like your own desk, your most frequently used items should be on the desktop so you can quickly access them to begin work. Those items that you use less frequently should be put away for easy access as needed, just as you might put papers in a drawer or on a nearby shelf.

Initially, the Windows 98 desktop displays six icons that represent the basic tools (described in the table below) needed by most users. Because the desktop can be customized to suit individual needs, your screen may have been modified from the default Windows 98 layout.

Icon		Description
My Computer	My Computer	Used to browse and manage items on a disk
My Documents	My Documents	A location where documents you create using an application program are stored on disk
Internet Explorer	Internet Explorer	Starts Internet Explorer or the associated Web browser
Recycle Bin	Recycle Bin	Holds deleted items you can permanently delete or restore
My Briefcase	My Briefcase	Used to transfer information between a desktop and portable computer
Outlook Express	Outlook Express	Accesses e-mail

Additionally the desktop can be displayed in two different views, **Web style view** (shown in Figure 1-2), or **Classic style view.** Web style view integrates the desktop with the World Wide Web by assuming the look and feel of the Internet Explorer program that is used to browse the Web. The **World Wide Web (Web or WWW)** is a part of the Internet that consists of information that is graphically displayed and interconnected by **hypertext links,** which allow users to quickly jump from one location to another. In this view the icons are underlined like hypertext links in a browser program and function in a similar manner.

Classic style view is the standard desktop view that was used in Windows 95, the previous version of Windows. Visually, Classic style view does not display the desktop icons with underlines to make them appear like hypertext links. Also, in Classic style features operate slightly differently. Figure 1-3 on the next page shows the desktop in classic style view.

FIGURE 1-3

icons in
Classic style
view

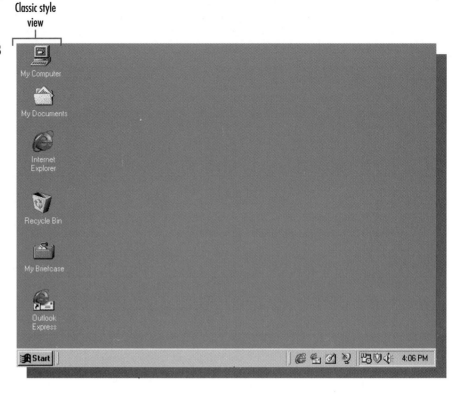

Finally, your computer may be set up to display the Active Desktop interface, which lets you put active content on your desktop. **Active content** is content from Web pages or a channel that changes on your screen, such as a stock ticker or weather map. A **channel** is a Web site designed to deliver content from the Internet to your computer. The Channel Bar and boxes displaying active content may be displayed on your desktop if this feature is on. For now, do not be concerned about the view you are using as you will learn to change the view shortly. Figure 1-4 on the next page shows how the desktop may appear if the Active Desktop interface is displayed.

FIGURE 1-4

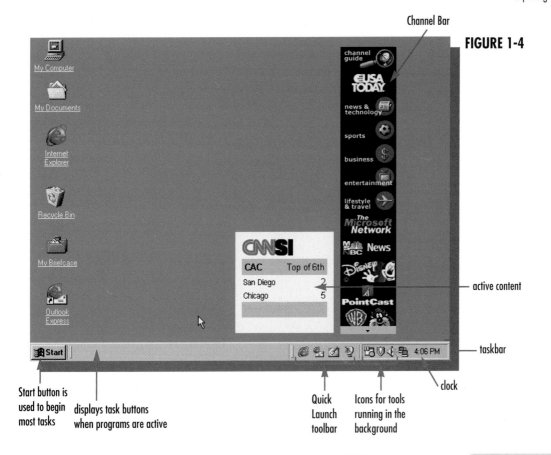

Channel Bar

active content

taskbar

clock

Start button is used to begin most tasks

displays task buttons when programs are active

Quick Launch toolbar

Icons for tools running in the background

At the bottom of the desktop screen is the **taskbar.** The [Start] button on the left end of the bar is used to start a program, open a document, get help, find information, and change system settings. A **button** is a common Windows feature that is used to access a feature. Buttons are square or rectangular shaped and appear depressed when selected, indicating they are in use. The center of the taskbar is currently blank. It will display **task buttons** representing currently active tasks as you use Windows, making switching between tasks easy. The clock icon on the right end of the taskbar displays the time as maintained by your computer. To the left of the clock are several icons that indicate those tools that are automatically started when you turn on your computer and are running in the background, such as a speaker if your system includes audio hardware. This area also temporarily displays icons while a tool is in use, such as a printer when printing is in progress.

In addition, the taskbar can display several different **toolbars.** Toolbars contain buttons that provide shortcuts to starting programs or using common features and commands. Toolbars are commonly found in all Windows applications. The default Windows 98 setup displays the Quick Launch toolbar in the taskbar. This toolbar contains buttons to start different elements of the Microsoft Internet Explorer Web browser program that is included with the Windows 98 operating system. It also contains a very handy ![show desktop icon] show desktop button that you will learn about shortly.

You will learn how to use a button shortly.

Your taskbar may display different icons than those shown in Figure 1-4.

starts Internet Explorer

starts Outlook Express

shows the desktop

accesses Microsoft channels

Using the Mouse

The arrow-shaped symbol on your screen is the **mouse pointer.** It is used to interact with objects on the screen and is controlled by the hardware device called a **mouse** that is attached to your computer.

Most commonly the mouse is a hand-held device that you move across the surface of your desk. A rubber-coated ball on the bottom of the mouse moves as you move the mouse. The ball's movement is translated into signals that tell the computer how to move the onscreen pointer. The direction the ball moves controls the direction the pointer moves on the screen.

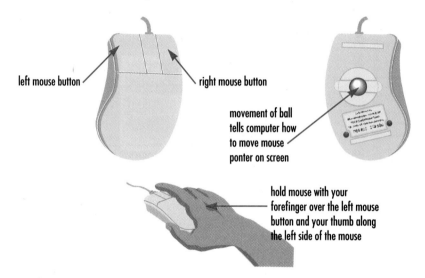

left mouse button

right mouse button

movement of ball tells computer how to move mouse ponter on screen

hold mouse with your forefinger over the left mouse button and your thumb along the left side of the mouse

Some computers use a track ball, a stick, or a touch pad to move the mouse pointer. The direction that you move the ball or stick with your fingertips or drag your finger on the pad is the direction the mouse pointer moves on the screen.

The mouse pointer changes shape on the screen depending on what it is pointing to. Some of the most common shapes are shown in the table below.

Pointer Shape	Meaning
⇖	Normal select
👆	Link select
⌛	Busy
⊘	Area is not available
⇖?	Displays Help on selected item
↔ ↕	Horizontal/vertical resize
⬉	Diagonal resize

On top of the mouse are two or three buttons that are used to choose items on the screen. If your system has a stick, ball, or touch pad, the buttons are located adjacent to the device. The buttons are used to **point, click, double-click,** and **drag.** These mouse actions are described in the table below.

When three buttons are available, the middle button can be programmed as the double-click button.

Throughout the labs, "click" means to use the left mouse button. If the right mouse button is to be used, the directions will tell you to right-click on the item.

Action	Description
Point	Move the mouse so the mouse pointer is positioned on the item you want to use.
Click	Press and release a mouse button. The left mouse button is the primary button that is used for most tasks.
Double-click	Quickly press and release the left mouse button twice.
Drag	Move the mouse while holding down a mouse button.

■ Move the mouse in all directions (up, down, left, and right) and note the movement of the mouse pointer.

■ Point to [My Computer].

Your screen should be similar to Figure 1-5.

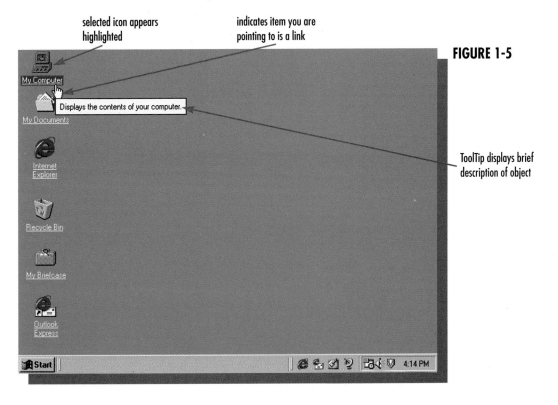

selected icon appears highlighted

indicates item you are pointing to is a link

ToolTip displays brief description of object

FIGURE 1-5

If you are using Classic style view, the mouse pointer is a ⬧ and you must click on the icon to select it.

The pointer on the screen moved in the direction you moved the mouse and currently appears as a 🖑. The icon appears highlighted, indicating it is the selected item and ready to be used. Many icons and most toolbar buttons will display a **ToolTip** containing a brief description of the item when you rest the mouse pointer on the item for a moment. You will find that ToolTips are used throughout Windows programs to quickly provide information about the tool you are pointing to.

- ■ Point to 📁 to view its ToolTip.
  My Documents

- ■ Point to each of the buttons on the taskbar to view their ToolTips.

Using the Start Menu

As you learn about Windows 98, you will find there are many ways to perform the same task. However, using the 🪟 Start button is one of the best places to learn how to use Windows 98. It provides quick and easy access to most features you will use frequently.

- ■ Click 🪟 Start.

Your screen should be similar to Figure 1-6.

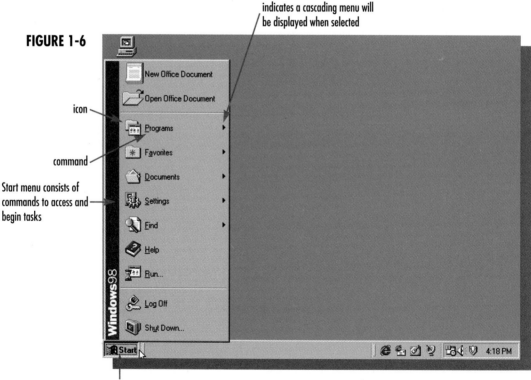

FIGURE 1-6

indicates a cascading menu will be displayed when selected

icon

command

Start menu consists of commands to access and begin tasks

clicking this button opens the Start menu

Clicking 🪟 Start opens the Start menu. The Start menu is a special Windows 98 menu that is used to access and begin all activities you want to perform on the computer. It is one of many menus you will see in Windows 98.

Concept 3: Menu

A **menu** is one of many methods you can use to tell a program what you want it to do. When opened a menu displays a list of commands. Most menus appear in a **menu bar** across the top of the screen. Other menus pop up when you right-click (click the right mouse button) on an item or on the desktop. This type of menu is called a **shortcut menu.** The options in the shortcut menu reflect the most frequently used commands for the item you clicked on.

Menus are everywhere in Windows 98, but they all operate in the same way. Once a menu is open, you can *select* a command from the menu by pointing to it. A colored highlight bar, called the **selection cursor,** appears over the selected command. If the selected command line displays a ▶, a submenu of commands automatically appears when the command is selected. This is commonly called a **cascading menu.** Then to *choose* a command you click on it. When the command is chosen, the associated action is performed. If the number of commands is larger than the length of the panel, a **scrolling menu** is used. This menu allows you to bring additional commands into view using the

[▲   ] and [▼   ] scroll buttons.

Menus may include the following features (not all menus include all features):

Feature	Meaning
Ellipses (...)	Indicates a dialog box will be displayed.
▶	Indicates a cascading menu will be displayed.
Dimmed command	Indicates the command is not available for selection until certain other conditions are met.
Shortcut key	A key or key combination that can be used to execute a command without using the menu.
Check mark (✔)	Indicates a toggle type of command: selecting it turns the feature on or off. A ✔ indicates the feature is on.
Bullet (●)	Indicates that the commands in that group are mutually exclusive: only one can be selected. The bullet indicates the currently selected feature.

You can also type the underlined command letter to select or choose a command. If the command is already selected, you can press [Enter] to choose it.

Holding down [Shift] while right-clicking an object displays a shortcut menu of every available command for that object.

The basic Start menu consists of a list of nine commands that are used to start programs, open documents, customize your system, get Help, search for items on your computer, and more. The icons to the left of each command are

Depending on your system setup, your Start menu may display additional commands.

graphic representations of the feature. The commands and what they are used for are described briefly in the table below.

Command	Used to
📁 Programs	Start programs
✱ Favorites	Open your favorite Web sites or folders
📁 Documents	Open recently used documents
⚙ Settings	Change or view the computer system settings
🔍 Find	Search for documents, Web pages, and people
📖 Help	Obtain direct access to the Help feature
🖥 Run	Start a program by specifying the name and location of the program
🔑 Log Off	Log off the computer so someone else can use it
🖥 Shut Down	Shut down or restart the computer

■ Point to the Shut Down command and slide the mouse pointer up the menu to select the Log Off, Run, Help, and Find commands.

■ Slide the mouse pointer to the right and point to the commands in the Find submenu.

Your screen should be similar to Figure 1-7.

FIGURE 1-7

selection cursor highlights currently selected commands

cascading menu

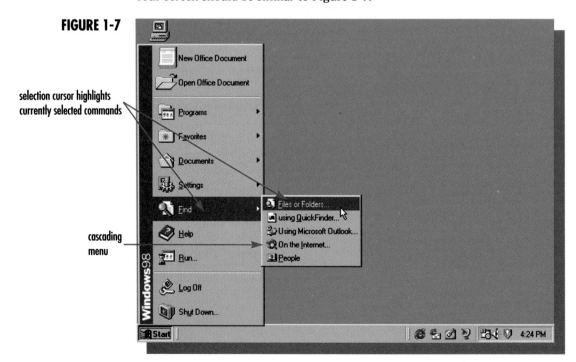

The selection cursor appears over each command as you point to it. Because an arrowhead symbol appears next to the Find command, it displays a cascading menu of additional commands when it is selected.

■ Point to the Settings, Documents, Favorites, and Programs commands to see the submenus associated with each.

■ Click outside the Start menu box on a blank area of the desktop to close the menu.

Developing the skill for moving the mouse and correctly positioning the pointer takes some time. If you accidentally find yourself in the wrong location or in a command that you did not intend to select, cancel the selected menu as you did above and try again.

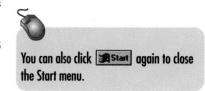

You can also click 🟦Start again to close the Start menu.

Starting the Help Program

Next you will use the Start menu to open the Windows 98 Help program. As you are learning to use a program, you will find that using the program's **Help** command provides an invaluable source of information about commands and procedures.

■ Open the Start menu again.

■ Click 📖 <u>H</u>elp.

Your screen should be similar to Figure 1-8.

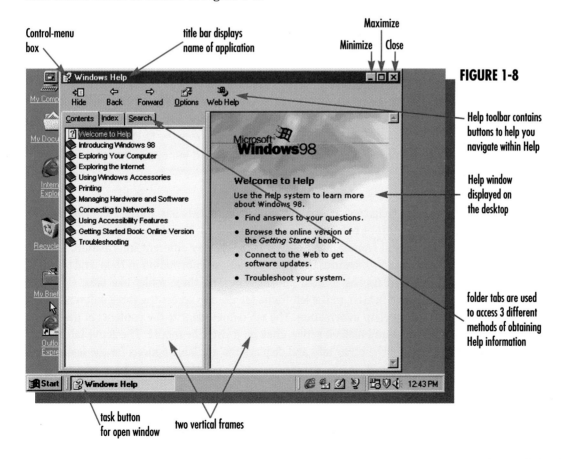

Control-menu box

title bar displays name of application

Minimize

Maximize

Close

FIGURE 1-8

Help toolbar contains buttons to help you navigate within Help

Help window displayed on the desktop

folder tabs are used to access 3 different methods of obtaining Help information

task button for open window

two vertical frames

You have executed the Help command, the Start menu is closed, and the Windows 98 Help program is started and displayed in a window on the desktop. The taskbar displays a task button for the open window.

> ### Concept 4: Window
>
> A **window** is a rectangular section on the screen that is used to display information and other programs. Each program that you open is displayed in its own window. Multiple programs, each in its own window, can be open at the same time. This makes it easy to switch from one project to another as you work.

Using the Help Window

All windows have a **title bar** located at the top of the window that displays the program name, in this case Windows Help. It also contains the four buttons described below.

Button	Description
Control-menu box	When opened, displays the Control menu consisting of a list of commands that are used to move, size, and otherwise control the window.
Minimize button	Used to reduce a window to its smallest size.
Maximize/Restore buttons	Used to enlarge a window to its maximum size. Changes to when maximized to allow you to return the window to its previous size.
Close button	Used to exit the application running in the window and to close the window.

The Help toolbar is displayed below the title bar. In the Help window, the toolbar buttons help you navigate within Help. The Help window is divided into two vertical **frames,** each of which can display different information. The left frame contains features that help you access information in Help, and the right frame displays the located information. The three folder-like **tabs,** Contents, Index, and Search, in the left frame are used to access the three different means of getting Help information. The tab names identify the contents of the tab. To open a tab and make it active, click on it with the mouse. The active tab appears in front of the other tabs and displays the available options for the feature.

■   If the Contents tab is not the active tab, click on it.

The Contents tab (shown in Figure 1-8) is active and displays a table of contents listing of topics in Help. Clicking on an item preceded with a ◆ opens a "chapter," which expands to display additional chapters or specific Help topics. Chapters are preceded with a ◆ icon and topics with a [?] icon.

- ■ Click Introducing Windows 98.

- ■ Click How to Use Help.

- ■ Click Find a topic.

The Help window on your screen should be similar to Figure 1-9.

active tab appears in front of other tabs and its contents are displayed in the frame

right frame displays information on the selected topic

FIGURE 1-9

open book indicates expanded chapter

selected topic

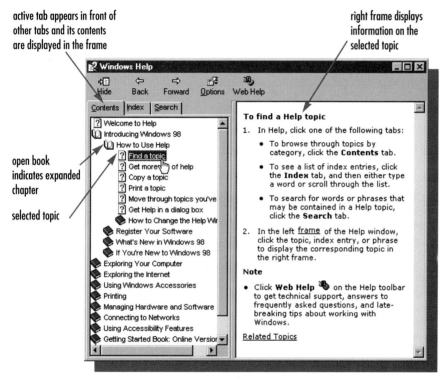

The book icon appears as an open book 📖 when expanded, and subordinate chapters and topics appear indented as in an outline. The right frame displays information about the selected topic.

- ■ Read the Help information on how to find a Help topic.

- ■ Click on the underlined word <u>frame</u>.

The Help window on your screen should be similar to Figure 1-10.

FIGURE 1-10

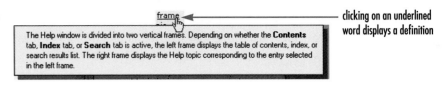

clicking on an underlined word displays a definition

A pop-up box containing a description of how frames operate is displayed. Whenever you see an underlined word in a Help topic, you can click on it to see a definition of the term.

■ Click on the pop-up box to clear it.

Using the Scroll Bar

Next you want to find more information about using Help and the desktop. To locate information on a specific topic, you use the Index tab.

■ Click Index.

The Help window on your screen should be similar to Figure 1-11.

FIGURE 1-11

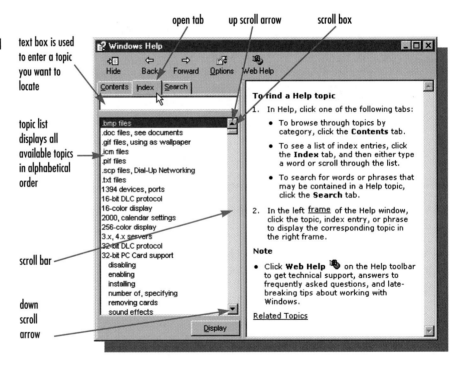

text box is used to enter a topic you want to locate

topic list displays all available topics in alphabetical order

scroll bar

down scroll arrow

The Index tab consists of a **text box** where you can type a word or phrase that best describes the topic you want to locate. Below that is a **list box** displaying a complete list of Help topics in alphabetical order. The topic list contains more topics than can be displayed at one time. A **scroll bar** is used with a mouse to bring additional lines of information into view in a space. Scroll bars can run vertically along the right side or horizontally along the bottom. The vertical scroll bar is used to move vertically and the horizontal scroll bar moves horizontally in the space. The scroll bar consists of **scroll arrows** and a **scroll box.** Clicking the arrows moves the information in the direction of the arrows, allowing new topics to be displayed in the space.

You can also move to a general location within the area by dragging the scroll box up or down the scroll bar. The location of the scroll box on the scroll bar indicates your relative position within the area of available information. In many scroll bars, the size of the scroll box also indicates the relative amount of information available. For example, a small box indicates that only a small amount of the total available information is displayed, whereas a large box indicates that almost all or a large portion of the total amount of available information is displayed.

To bring more topics into view, you will scroll the list using the scroll bar.

- Click ▼ five times.

- To continuously scroll the list, point to ▼ and hold down the left mouse button for a few seconds

- Click ▲ several times.

The list of topics has moved up and down line by line, allowing new topics to be displayed in the list box. Did you notice the movement of the scroll box as you scrolled the list? It moves up or down along the scroll bar to show your relative location within the list. Clicking above or below the scroll box moves the list up or down a box full of topics at a time, and dragging the scroll box moves to a general location within the list.

- Click on the scroll bar below the scroll box several times.

- Drag the scroll box to the lower third of the scroll bar.

- Click above the scroll box.

- Using the scroll bar, locate the topic "clearing Help contents from screen."

- Double-click on this topic to display it.

If there is no scroll box in the scroll bar, this indicates the entire topic is visible in the window.

To drag, hold down the left mouse button while moving the mouse.

You could also click on the topic to select it and then click [Display] to display it.

The Help window on your screen should be similar to Figure 1-12.

FIGURE 1-12

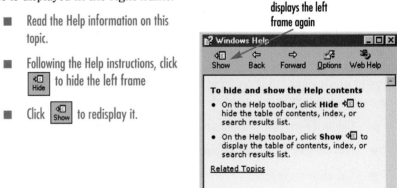

The selected topic appears in the text box while the information about the topic is displayed in the right frame.

- Read the Help information on this topic.

- Following the Help instructions, click
  [Hide] to hide the left frame

- Click [Show] to redisplay it.

Using a Text Box

An easier way to move to a topic in the Index list is to type the first few letters of the topic in the text box. You will use this method to find out more about the My Computer icon on the desktop. The text box must be active before you can type information in it. When active, a blinking vertical bar called the **insertion point** is displayed or the information in the text box is highlighted. To activate the text box,

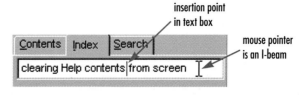

insertion point
in text box

mouse pointer
is an I-beam

- Click in the text box.

The insertion point appears in the text box within the text where you were pointing when you clicked the mouse. In addition, the mouse pointer appears as an I-beam when it is in the text box. It is used to position the insertion point.

Before you can type the new text, you need to clear the current entry. To do this you could use [Backspace] or [Del] to remove each character one character at a time. Another way is to select or highlight the entry and then type the new entry. To select text you drag the mouse pointer from one end of the entry to the other.

- Select the text in the text box.

selected text
appears highlighted

The entire entry appears highlighted, indicating that it is selected. Now, as soon as you begin typing, the existing entry will be cleared and replaced by the text you are typing. As you type each letter, the list will scroll to the topic that most closely matches the letters you enter and highlight the topic.

- Type **my c**

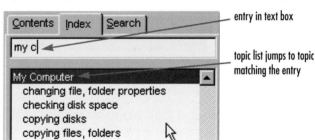

entry in text box

topic list jumps to topic
matching the entry

The selection cursor now highlights the first topic in the list that starts with "my c": My Computer. Since you have located the topic you want, you do not need to type the rest of the word.

- Double-click the My Computer topic.

Your screen should be similar to Figure 1-13.

FIGURE 1-13

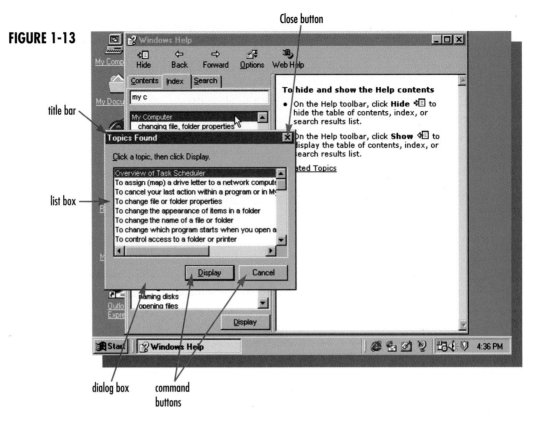

A list of subtopics under the My Computer topic is displayed in a dialog box.

Using Dialog Boxes

Because there is more than one item of information available on this topic, the list of topics to select from is displayed in a dialog box.

Concept 5: Dialog Box

A **dialog box** is a window that is displayed whenever the program requires additional information to complete a task. All dialog boxes have a title bar at the top, which displays a name identifying the contents of the dialog box, and a ☒ button that is used to close the box. Inside the dialog box are command buttons and areas to select or specify the needed information. The features shown in the table below may be found in dialog boxes; however, not all features are found in every dialog box. Some features, such as text boxes and scroll bars, are also found in windows and menus. Others are only found in dialog boxes.

Feature	Meaning
What's This [?]	Displays Help on dialog box options.
Text box `clearing Help contents from screen`	An area where you type in the requested information.
Drop-down list box `My Computer ▼`	A text box that displays the currently selected item and a ▼ button. Clicking the ▼ button displays a drop-down list of items from which you can select, or you can type the information in the text box.
Option button ⊙	Used to select from a group of options. The selected option displays a black dot in the option button. Only one option can be selected from a list of option buttons.
Check box ☑	Used to select from a group of options. The selected option displays a ✔. More than one option can be selected from a list of check box options.
List box	A box displaying a list of information from which you can select.
Sliding control `Slow ——┃—— Fast`	Dragging the lever in the control increases or decreases the related setting, such as volume.
Command button `OK`	Instructs Windows to carry out the instructions on the button. The two most common command buttons are `OK` and `Cancel`. Other buttons you will see are `Close`, `Help`, `Options...`, `Setup...`, `Display`, and `Settings...`.

- Scroll the list and select "To see what's on your computer."
- Click `Display`.
- Read the information on this topic.

You could also double-click the topic to display it.

Your screen should be similar to Figure 1-14.

FIGURE 1-14

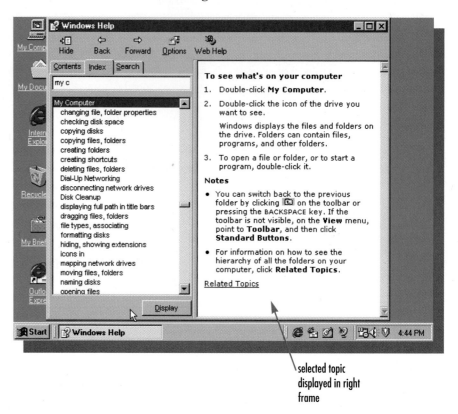

selected topic
displayed in right
frame

The dialog box is closed, and the information on the selected topic is displayed in the right frame.

Now that you have learned how to use the Start menu and many window and dialog box features, if your computer is using Classic view you will change to Web style view.

■ If necessary, choose **Start** /**S**ettings/**F**older Options/**W**eb Style/ OK .

Note: If you are running short on lab time, you can quit before beginning Part 2. To do this, close the Help window, then follow the directions to quit Windows 98 on page WN48. When you begin Part 2, display the Help window shown in Figure 1-14 and switch to Web style view if necessary.

Part 2

Opening a Second Window

Next you decide to follow the Help instructions on this topic to see what is on your computer. You will keep the Help window open so you can see the directions while performing the actions.

- Click ⟨Hide⟩ .

- Click ⟨My Computer⟩ .

Your screen should be similar to Figure 1-15.

> The Help instructions tell you to double-click the icon because they are written for Classic style view users.

> Do not be concerned that your windows are in a different location or size on the desktop. You will learn about moving and sizing windows shortly.

used to move and size toolbars and menu bars   active window title bar is colored

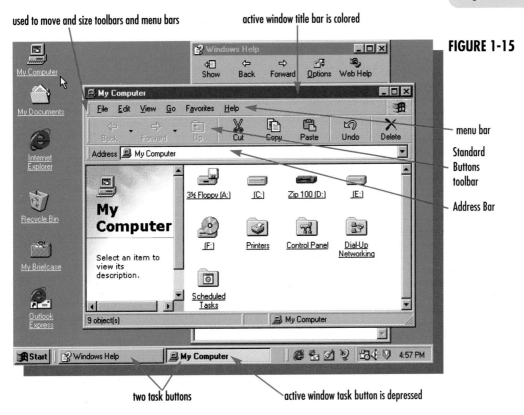

FIGURE 1-15

menu bar

Standard Buttons toolbar

Address Bar

two task buttons   active window task button is depressed

A second window, My Computer, is open on the desktop, and the taskbar displays a task button for this open window. There are now two programs running at the same time, Help and My Computer. The capability to run multiple programs at the same time is called **multitasking.** This makes using your computer more like you would actually work, allowing you to switch easily between tasks without having to put one away before beginning the other.

> The task buttons resize themselves automatically depending on the number of open tasks.

The My Computer window is the **active window,** the window that is currently in use. You can tell it is the active window because the task button appears depressed and the window title bar is colored. Multiple windows can be open on the desktop at once, but only one window is active at a time.

When a new window is opened, it appears in the size in which it was last used and in any location on the desktop. The newly open window is automatically the active window and appears on top of other open windows on the desktop. To see a window that is below another window and make it the active window, you can click on the window's task button or anywhere on the window if it is visible.

■ To make the Help window active, click anywhere in the Help window or click the Help task button.

Now the active window is on top and the entire Help window is visible again.

■ Make the My Computer window active again.

Exploring the My Computer Window

The My Computer window is used to view the information stored as files on your computer.

Concept 6: File

The information a computer uses is stored electronically as a variety of different **files** on a disk. Program files contain the software instructions that you use to run the program. The information you create while using an application program is stored in data files. For example, if you write a letter to a friend using an application program, the contents of the letter are stored as a data file.

Like all windows, the My Computer window title bar displays the name of the program it contains. Below the title bar is a menu bar containing six menus that when selected display drop-down menus of commands. The menus in a menu bar contain the same features and operate just like the Start menu. The general features in each menu are described in the following table.

Menu	Use
File	Used to perform tasks related to files, such as renaming and deleting.
Edit	Used to undo, cut, copy, paste, and select objects within the displayed window.
View	Controls the display of features such as toolbars, icon arrangement, and the status bar.
Go	Used to navigate and to open supplementary applications.
Favorites	Lists of user-defined favorite Web sites and folders.
Help	Opens Windows 98 Help.

- Click on the File menu to display the drop-down menu.

- Point to each of the five other menus to display their drop-down menus.

- Click on a blank area in the window to close the menu bar.

By default the My Computer window displays two toolbars, Standard Buttons and Address Bar, below the menu bar. (See Figure 1-15.) The buttons on the Standard Buttons toolbar activate the most commonly used menu commands and features in My Computer. The Address Bar contains a text box that displays the current location you are viewing. You can also use it to enter a location to go to by typing the location address in the text box. In addition, a Links toolbar containing buttons to WWW sites may be displayed.

> You will learn more about the Address Bar in Lab 2.

- If necessary, choose **V**iew/**T**oolbars/**S**tandard Buttons to display the Standard Buttons toolbar.

- In a similar manner, if necessary, display the Address Bar and hide the Links toolbar.

> A ✔ next to a menu option means it is selected.

Notice the ▌ bar to the left of each toolbar. Dragging this bar up or down allows you to change the order of the toolbars. If multiple toolbars share the same row, dragging the bar left or right adjusts the size of the toolbar. If you right-click on a toolbar, the toolbar shortcut menu is displayed. Using this menu you can specify which toolbars are displayed and turn on or off the display of the button labels to allow more space to display page content. Next you will try out several of these features.

> Double-clicking ▌ when multiple toolbars share the same row minimizes or maximizes the toolbar size.

- Right-click on any toolbar to display the shortcut menu.

- Choose **T**ext Labels.

> The menu equivalent is **V**iew/**T**oolbars/**T**ext Labels.

Now the buttons on the Standard Buttons

toolbar are smaller and do not display the button name. You can display the button name by pointing to the button.

- Point to any button on the Standard Buttons toolbar to see the ToolTip displaying the button name.

- Right-click on any toolbar and select Text Labels to redisplay the button names.

- Display the toolbar shortcut menu again and select Standard Buttons to hide the toolbar.

- Redisplay the Standard Buttons toolbar.

- Point to the ▌ of the Address Bar and drag it up into the middle of the Standard Buttons toolbar.

- Double-click the ▌ of the Address Bar to maximize the toolbar.

- Drag the ▌ of the Address Bar to the right until each bar occupies approximately half the row space.

- Drag the ▌ of the Address Bar back down to the space below the Standard Buttons toolbar.

As you can see, by hiding and moving toolbars and changing the text label display, you can customize the appearance of the toolbars and minimize the space they use.

The My Computer Window on your screen should again be similar to Figure 1-16.

The menu equivalent is <u>V</u>iew/<u>T</u>oolbars/<u>S</u>tandard Buttons.

The mouse pointer appears as ←→ when you point to the ▌ of any toolbar and as ◄▌► when you drag it.

FIGURE 1-16

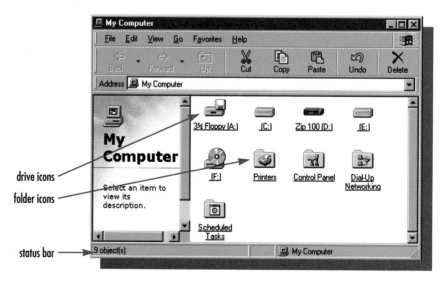

drive icons

folder icons

status bar

The display area of the My Computer window is divided into two frames. The left frame currently provides directions on how to use the window. The right frame displays icons representing various features associated with your computer. Some or all of the items shown in the table below may be displayed in your My Computer window.

If your window is too small, the left frame may not be displayed.

If your left frame displays different information than in Figure 1-16, use **V**iew/**E**xplorer Bar/**N**one.

Icon	Representation
	3.5-inch floppy-disk drive
	Hard-disk drive
	Network drive
	CD-ROM drive
	Zip drive

In addition, there are several folder icons displayed.

Concept 7: Folder

A **folder** is a named area on a disk that is used to store related subfolders and files. Folders are used to organize the information you store on a disk. This is similar to how you in store related information in separate folders in a file drawer. Using folders makes it easier to locate files.

You will learn more about folders in Lab 2.

At the bottom of the window a **status bar** is displayed. The information displayed in the status bar varies with the program you are using and the task being performed. The purpose of the status bar is to advise you of the status of different program conditions and features as you use the program. Currently the status bar tells you the number of items, called **objects,** in the window.

If the status bar is not displayed, choose **V**iew/**S**tatus Bar to turn it on.

Moving and Sizing Windows

Sometimes the location and size of a window when it opens are not convenient for what you want to do. To make the desktop more workable, you can move and size windows.

> You cannot change the size of a dialog box.

Concept 8: Moving and Sizing Windows

Moving and sizing windows allows you to conveniently view information on your desktop. A window or a dialog box can be moved anywhere on the desktop. Moving a window simply displays the window at another location on the desktop. It does not change the size of the window. To move a window or dialog box, simply point to the title bar and drag the window to the new location on the desktop.

You can also adjust the size of a window to just about any size you want. A window can be **minimized** to its smallest size using the ▭ Minimize button, or **maximized** to its largest size using the ▣ Maximize button. A maximized window can then be **restored** to its previous size using the ▣ Restore button. In addition, a window can be custom sized by pointing to the window border and dragging the border in the direction you want to size it. Dragging inward decreases the size and dragging outward increases the size. Dragging a corner increases or decreases the size of the two adjoining borders while maintaining the window proportions.

You will try out these features by moving and sizing the two open windows on your desktop.

- ■ Point to the My Computer window title bar and drag to move the left edge of the window even with the left edge of the desktop.

- ■ In a similar manner, drag the Help window to the right edge of the desktop.

Your screen should be similar to Figure 1-17.

window moved to the left

FIGURE 1-17

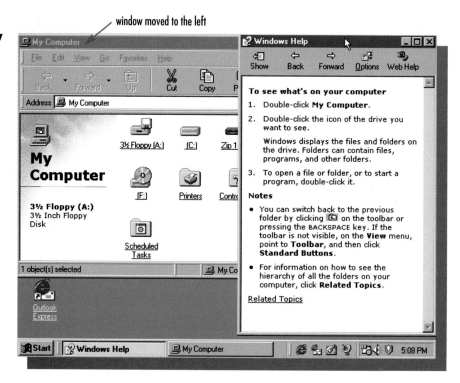

Now you can see much more of both windows. Next, to see the entire My Computer window contents, you will maximize the window.

■ Make the My Computer window active.

■ Click ⬜ Maximize in the My Computer window title bar.

The My Computer window now occupies the entire desktop.

When a window is maximized, the Maximize button changes to 🗗 Restore. This button is used to return a window to its previous size.

■ Click 🗗 Restore.

You can also custom size and shape a window by adjusting the window borders. When you point to a border or corner, the mouse pointer changes to a two-headed arrow ↔. The directions in which the arrowheads point indicate the direction in which you can drag the border or corner.

■ Point to a corner of the My Computer window and, when the pointer changes to ↙, drag the mouse inward or outward until the window size is as in Figure 1-18.

Your screen should be similar to Figure 1-18.

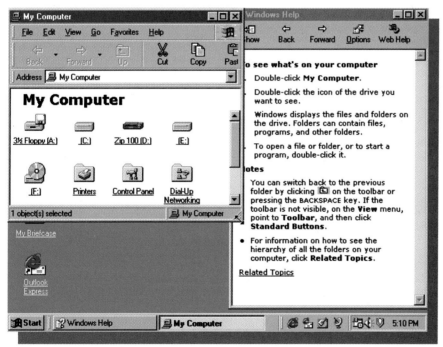

FIGURE 1-18

Once a window has been custom sized, the only way to return it to the original size is by dragging the borders again.

■ Return the window to its original size.

Often you will want to keep a window open for future reference, but you do not want it to occupy space on the desktop. To do this, you can minimize the window.

You can also click the active window's task button to minimize the window.

■ Click 🔲 Minimize in the My Computer window title bar.

Your screen should be similar to Figure 1-19.

FIGURE 1-19

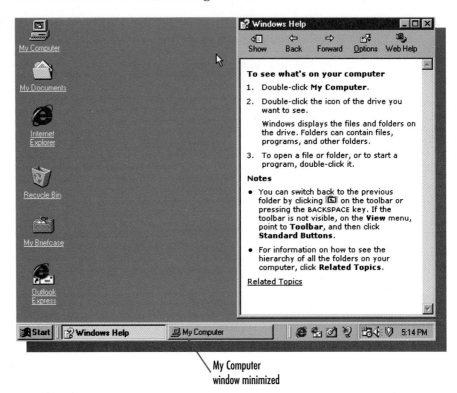

My Computer
window minimized

The window is no longer displayed on the desktop. The My Computer button in the taskbar, however, is still displayed. This indicates the window is still open, but minimized. To redisplay the window, simply click on its taskbar button.

■ Click 🖳 My Computer .

The My Computer window is redisplayed on the desktop in the size and location it last appeared.

Arranging Windows

In addition to sizing and moving windows, you can use Windows 98's window-arranging features.

Concept 9: Arranging Windows

There are two ways to arrange windows on the desktop, **cascade** and **tile.**

Feature	Description
Cascade	Layers open windows, displaying the active window fully and only the title bars of all other open windows behind it.
Tile	Resizes each open window and arranges the windows vertically or horizontally on the desktop.

| cascade | tile horizontally | tile vertically |

Cascading windows is useful if you want to work primarily in one window but you want to see the titles of other open windows. Tiling is most useful when you want to work in several applications simultaneously, because it allows you to quickly see the contents of all open windows and move between them. However, the greater the number of open windows, the smaller is the space available to display the tiled window contents.

To access the menu of options that allow you to arrange windows,

■ Right-click on any blank area of the taskbar.

The taskbar shortcut menu is displayed. This shortcut menu contains commands associated with taskbar settings and arranging open windows. To cascade the open windows,

■ Choose Cascade Windows.

Your shortcut menu may display additional options, depending upon the location in the taskbar where you right-clicked.

Reminder: Click on a command to choose it.

Your screen should be similar to Figure 1-20.

FIGURE 1-20

two cascaded windows

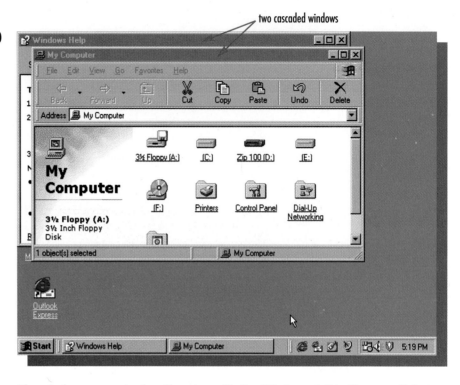

Windows that are minimized are not arranged.

The windows are resized and overlap with the title bars visible. You can click on any visible part of the window to make it active.

■ Make the Help window active.

The Help window is pulled to the front of the stack and covers the other cascaded window.

To restore the window size and arrangement as it was prior to cascading the windows, you can use the Undo feature.

Concept 10: Undo

The **Undo** feature allows you to reverse your last action or command. This feature is available in most software application programs. In some programs you can undo multiple actions, up to a certain limit. Others, as in Windows 98, allow you to undo only your last action. You will find that some actions you perform cannot be undone. If the Undo command is unavailable, it appears dimmed and you cannot cancel your last action.

The Undo option appears in the taskbar shortcut menu only after windows have been arranged.

■ Display the taskbar shortcut menu.

■ Choose <u>U</u>ndo Cascade.

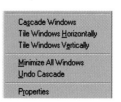

The windows are arranged and sized again as they were before using the Cascade command. If you do not undo the arrangement before switching to another arrangement, the windows remain in the size and position set by the second arrangement and cannot be returned to their original size without custom sizing and moving the windows.

To arrange the windows on the desktop without overlapping,

■ Choose Tile Windows V̲ertically from the taskbar shortcut menu.

Your screen should be similar to Figure 1-21.

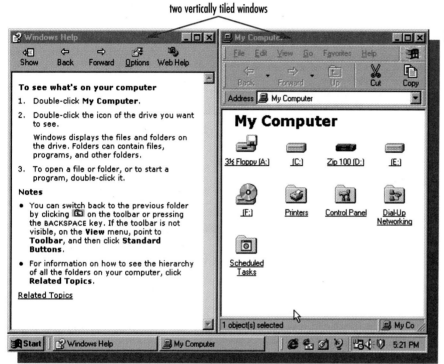

two vertically tiled windows

FIGURE 1-21

The two windows are vertically arranged on the desktop, each taking up one half of the vertical space.

Next you will undo this window arrangement and then tile the windows horizontally.

■ Choose U̲ndo Tile from the taskbar shortcut menu.

■ Choose Tile Windows H̲orizontally from the taskbar shortcut menu.

Your screen should be similar to Figure 1-22.

FIGURE 1-22

two horizontally
tiled windows

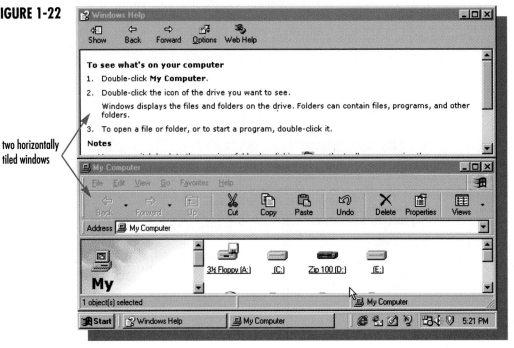

The two windows are horizontally arranged on the desktop, each taking up one half of the horizontal space.

■ Undo this window arrangement.

Finally, the Minimize All Windows command on the taskbar shortcut menu can be used to quickly minimize all open windows. In addition, the [icon] Show Desktop button on the Quick Launch toolbar in the taskbar can perform the same action.

■ Click [icon] Show Desktop or choose <u>M</u>inimize All Windows from the taskbar shortcut menu.

Your screen should be similar to Figure 1-23.

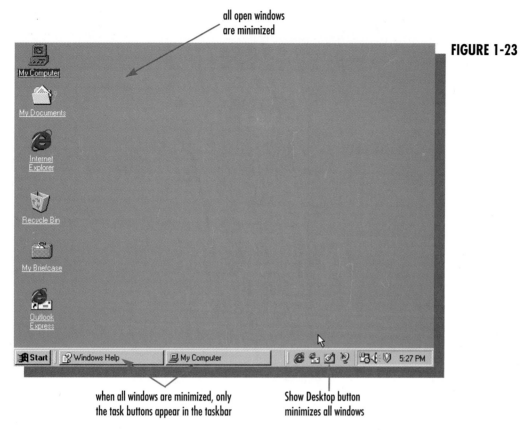

FIGURE 1-23

The desktop is cleared of all open windows. This is much quicker than minimizing each window individually.

Checking Disk Properties and Contents

Next you will use the My Computer window to see what is on your computer.

- Click ▤My Computer in the taskbar to display the My Computer window.

- Maximize the window.

- Point to the ▱ icon (or the appropriate hard drive for your system).
  [C:]

Your screen should be similar to Figure 1-24.

FIGURE 1-24

selected drive

properties of selected drive

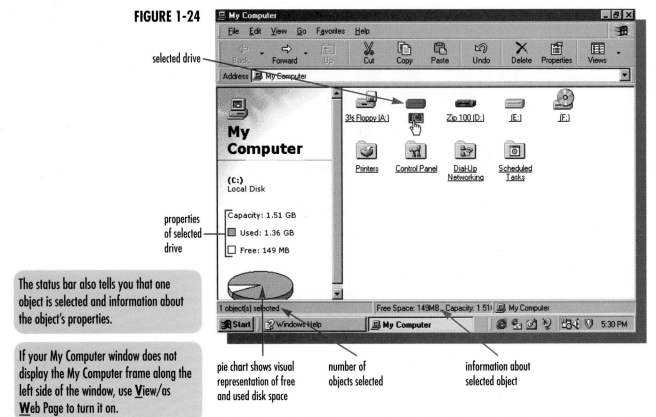

The status bar also tells you that one object is selected and information about the object's properties.

If your My Computer window does not display the My Computer frame along the left side of the window, use **V**iew/as **W**eb Page to turn it on.

pie chart shows visual representation of free and used disk space

number of objects selected

information about selected object

The hard drive icon is highlighted, indicating it is selected. The left frame displays some basic information about the properties of the disk.

Concept 11: Properties

Properties are the settings and attributes associated with an object on the screen, such as an icon. Just about all the objects on the desktop have properties associated with them. The desktop itself is an object that has properties. The properties can be viewed and changed if necessary to suit your needs.

The left frame tells you the total **capacity** or amount of data the disk is capable of holding. The capacity value should equal the amount of free and used space. The pie chart visually represents this information. To see more detailed information about the properties associated with the C drive, you can open the Properties dialog box.

■ Right-click (or the appropriate hard drive for your system).

■ Choose P**r**operties.

The Properties dialog box on your screen should be similar to Figure 1-25.

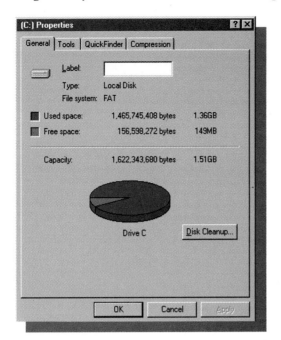

FIGURE 1-25

The General tab displays the same disk usage information in more detail.

■ Look through the other tabs to see what types of features you can use to modify the properties of the selected disk.

■ Click [OK] .

Choosing a drive icon displays the contents of the disk in that drive. To see the contents of your computer's hard drive,

■ Click [C:] (or the appropriate hard drive for your system).

The right frame displays the files and folders on the selected drive. They are identified by names that are descriptive of the contents of the file or folder. The folder names are listed first in alphabetical order and are preceded with folder icons 🗀. The individual files are listed following the folders, again in alphabetical order.

> The information in the Address Bar reflects your current location.

■ If necessary, scroll the window to view the files.

Your screen should be similar to Figure 1-26.

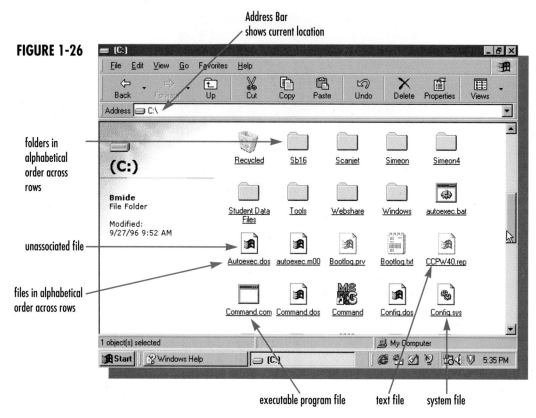

FIGURE 1-26

You will see many other kinds of icons that represent different types of files on your disk. The various file icons help you distinguish the type of file: a program file, an associated file, or another type of file (generally an unassociated document file). An **associated file** is a file that has a specific application program attached to it that will open when the file is opened. The table on the following page describes several of the file icons.

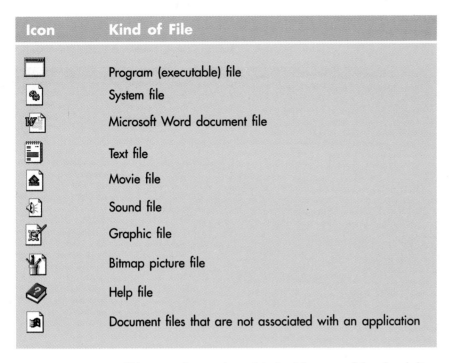

Icon	Kind of File
	Program (executable) file
	System file
	Microsoft Word document file
	Text file
	Movie file
	Sound file
	Graphic file
	Bitmap picture file
	Help file
	Document files that are not associated with an application

■ Point to several file icons and as you do, read the brief description of the selected object in the left frame.

Changing the Icon View

Icons in a window can be viewed or displayed in four different ways. These views change the icon size, display order, and the amount of information about the files and folders. Depending upon what you are doing, one view may be more helpful than another.

The View menu contains the commands to change views. In addition, many of these commands have toolbar button shortcuts that can be used instead of selecting from the menu. The ⊞ button is a **drop-down list button.** It consists of two parts: the ⊞ button, which applies the next option, and the ⋅ button, which displays a drop-down list of options.

> Another way to change the view is to select the command from the window's shortcut menu. This method is useful if the toolbar is not displayed.

■ Click ⋅ of ⊞ to open the Views drop-down list.

The four icon options change the view of the files and folders in the window. The Large Icons options should be selected, as this is the default setting. It displays a bullet to show it is the selected option. To change the view to display small icons,

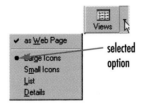

selected option

■ Choose Small Icons.

> The menu equivalent is View/Small Icons.

Your screen should be similar to Figure 1-27.

Views drop-down list button   click to display drop-down list

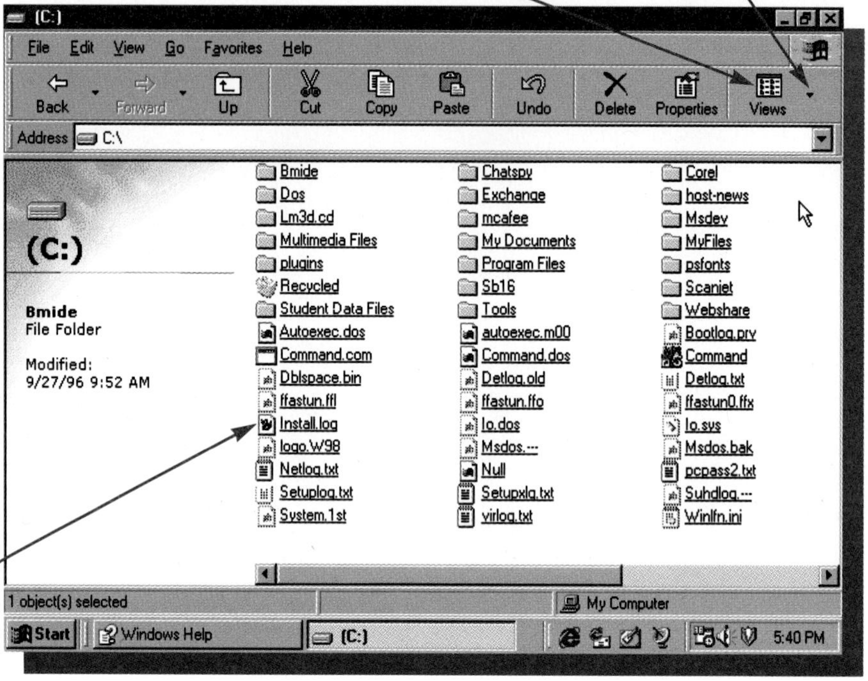

FIGURE 1-27

Small Icon view displays
small icons with name to
right of the icon

The icons appear in the same order, but many more folders and files can be displayed because the icon size is much smaller. The icon name appears to the right of the icon. The next view, List, is similar to the Small Icons view.

The menu equivalent is **V**iew/**L**ist.

■   Choose **L**ist from the [Views] button drop-down list.

The icons are the same size as in Small Icons view, but they are arranged alphabetically down columns rather than across rows in the window. The last view setting displays the file details, such as total file size, type, and date and time of creation. To see this view,

The menu equivalent is **V**iew/**D**etails.

■   Choose **D**etails from the [Views] button drop-down list.

Clicking [Views] cycles through all four views.

Your screen should be similar to Figure 1-28.

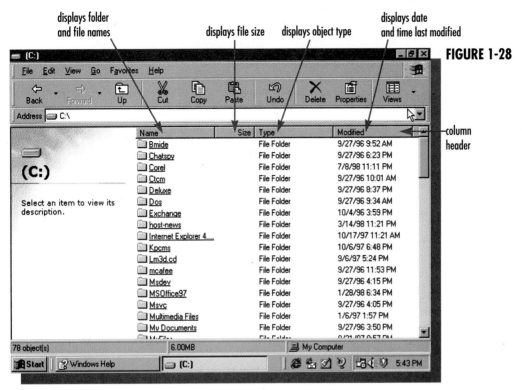

FIGURE 1-28

The names of the folders and files appear in a single column down the window, with the additional file information displayed in columns to the right. The columns are labeled with a column header. The columns display the file or folder name, the file size (in bytes), type of file, and date and time the file was last modified.

■ If necessary, scroll the window to see the file icons.

This additional information takes up a lot of space in the window, making it necessary to scroll the window to locate a file or folder that is not visible. Rather than use this view to see the file's details, you can display the details for an individual file by viewing the file's properties.

■ Select any file in the list.

■ Click .

You can drag the column header divider lines to increase or decrease the size of the columns.

The menu equivalent is **File/Properties**. This command is also available on the object's shortcut menu.

The Properties dialog box on your screen should be similar to Figure 1-29.

FIGURE 1-29

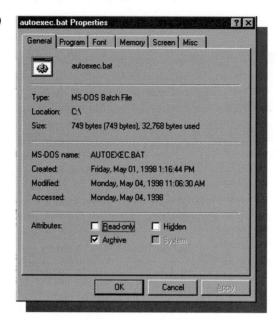

Depending upon the type of file you selected, the Properties dialog box may display many different tabs. However, the General tab is always displayed and contains much of the same information as in Details view, such as file size and date for the selected file.

■   After looking at the property information, close the dialog box.

Arranging Icons

Regardless of the view you are using, folders always appear first as a group, followed by files. Typically folders and files are displayed in alphabetical order by name. Sometimes, however, this order is not convenient. For example, you may be unable to remember the name of the file, but you can remember the date you last modified it. The Arrange Icons command in the View menu lets you select an arrangement that may be more convenient for the task you are performing.

The arrange icons options are described in this following table.

Option	Description
by **N**ame	Arranges items alphabetically by the file name.
by **T**ype	Arranges items alphabetically by file type.
by Si**z**e	Arranges items by file size.
by **D**ate	Arranges items by date modified.
Auto Arrange	Arranges items in window automatically as you change the size of the window.

To arrange the files by size rather than name,

■ Choose **V**iew/Arrange **I**cons/by Si**z**e.

Your screen should be similar to Figure 1-30.

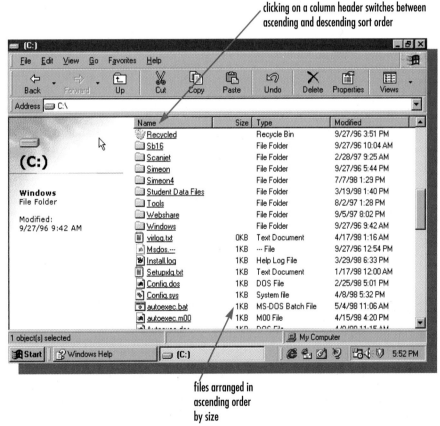

clicking on a column header switches between ascending and descending sort order

FIGURE 1-30

files arranged in ascending order by size

Looking at the Size column of information, you can see that the files are in ascending sorted order by file size.

Another way to change the sort order when using Details view is to click the column heads to switch the sort order between ascending and descending order. For example, clicking the Name column head changes the sort order to ascending or descending alphabetical order by name. In descending name order, files appear first before folders. To change the order back to display the icons in ascending alphabetical order by name,

- Click `Name`.
- Return the view to Large Icons.
- Click ⬅ Back.

The contents of the My Computer window you viewed previously are displayed again. Likewise, clicking ➡ Forward will display the contents of the next location you viewed after using ⬅ Back. You can also go directly to a previously viewed window by selecting the location from the button's drop-down list.

- Click ⬜ to restore the window to its original size.
- Click ✖ to close the My Computer window.

The My Computer task button is removed from the taskbar, indicating the program is no longer active.

- In a similar manner, close the Help window.

Shutting Down Windows 98

You can shut down Windows 98 in one of two ways. When you want to stop working and turn off your computer, use the Shut Down command in the Start menu. If, on the other hand, you share a computer and someone else will use it next, use the Log Off command. Follow the Log Off or Shut Down directions as specified by your instructor.

- Click **Start**.

If you are logging off,

- Choose 🔑 Log Off.
- Choose `Yes` from the dialog box to confirm that you want to log off.

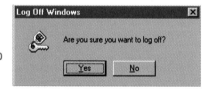

If you are shutting down the computer,

- Choose 💻 Shut Down.

The Shut Down Windows options are described in the following table.

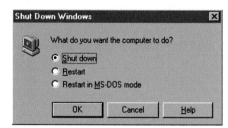

Side notes (left column):

The menu equivalent is **V**iew/**L**arge Icons.

The menu equivalent is **G**o/**B**ack, and the keyboard shortcut is `Alt` + `⬅`.

The menu equivalent is **G**o/**F**orward and the keyboard shortcut is `Alt` + `➡`.

The menu equivalent is **F**ile/**C**lose.

To avoid damaging files, always follow the procedure below to shut down Windows 98 before you turn off your computer.

Option	Effect
Shut down	Saves any settings you have changed in Windows 98, writes anything stored in memory to the hard disk, and prepares the computer to be turned off.
Restart	Saves any settings you have changed in Windows 98, writes anything stored in memory to the hard disk, and restarts the computer. This feature is commonly used when a program stops running and the system freezes up on you. This is called a **warm start.** A warm start does not perform a memory check, but it does initialize the equipment for use.
Restart in **M**S-DOS mode	Saves any settings you have changed in Windows 98, writes anything stored in memory to the hard disk, and restarts the computer in MS-DOS mode. This mode is needed to run DOS programs that will not run under Windows 98.

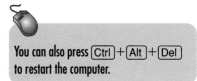

You can also press `Ctrl` + `Alt` + `Del` to restart the computer.

■ Select the option specified by your instructor.

■ Choose  to confirm your selection.

WARNING!

If you choose Shut Down the Computer, do not turn off your computer until you see the message indicating it is safe to do so.

LAB REVIEW

■ ■ ■ ■ ■ ■ ■ ■ ■ ■ ■ ■

Key Terms

active content   (WN10)
active window   (WN28)
application software   (WN2)
associated file   (WN42)
button   (WN11)
capacity   (WN41)
cascade   (WN35)
cascading menu   (WN15)
central processing unit
   (CPU)   (WN1)
channel   (WN10)
Classic style view   (WN9)
click   (WN13)
cold start   (WN6)
desktop   (WN8)
dialog box   (WN25)
double-click   (WN13)
drag   (WN13)
drop-down list button   (WN43)
file   (WN28)
folder   (WN31)
frame   (WN18)

graphical user interface
   (GUI)   (WN3)
Help   (WN17)
hypertext link   (WN9)
icon   (WN3)
insertion point   (WN22)
list box   (WN21)
maximize   (WN32)
menu   (WN15)
menu bar   (WN15)
minimize   (WN32)
mouse   (WN12)
mouse pointer   (WN12)
multitasking   (WN27)
object   (WN31)
operating system   (WN3)
point   (WN13)
program   (WN3)
properties   (WN40)
restore   (WN32)
scroll arrow   (WN21)
scroll bar   (WN21)

scroll box   (WN21)
scrolling menu   (WN15)
selection cursor   (WN15)
shortcut menu   (WN15)
software   (WN3)
system software (WN3)
status bar   (WN31)
tab   (WN18)
taskbar   (WN11)
task button   (WN11)
text box   (WN21)
tile   (WN35)
title bar   (WN18)
toolbar   (WN11)
ToolTip   (WN14)
Undo   (WN36)
warm start   (WN49)
Web style view   (WN9)
window   (WN3)
World Wide Web (WWW)   (WN9)

Command Summary

Command	Shortcut Key	Button	Action
Start Menu			
Help			Opens Windows Help program
Log Off			Prepare computer to be used by someone else
Sh**u**t Down			Safely shuts down computer before power is turned off
Settings/**F**older Options/**W**eb style			Changes desktop display to Web style view
My Computer			
File/Proper**t**ies		[Properties]	Displays properties associated with selected object
File/**C**lose		[✕]	Closes active window
View/**T**oolbars/**S**tandard Buttons			Turns on/off display of Standard Buttons toolbar
View/**T**oolbars/**A**ddress Bar			Turns on/off display of Address Bar

Command	Shortcut Key	Button	Action
View/**T**oolbars/**L**inks			Turns on/off display of Links toolbar
View/**T**oolbars/**T**ext Labels			Turns on/off display of text labels in Standard Buttons toolbar
View/**S**tatus Bar			Turns on/off display of status bar
View/**E**xplorer Bar/**N**one			Turns off display of Explorer Bars
View/as **W**eb page			Switches window view between Web style and Classic style
View/**Lar**ge Icons		Views	Displays objects with large icons
View/**Sm**all Icons		Views	Displays objects with small icons
View/**L**ist		Views	Displays objects in a list
View/**D**etails		Views	Displays all folder and file details
View/Arrange **I**cons/by **N**ame			Organizes icons alphabetically by name
View/Arrange **I**cons/by **T**ype			Organizes icons by type of files
View/Arrange **I**cons/by Si**z**e			Organizes icons by size of files
View/Arrange **I**cons/by **D**ate			Organizes icons by last modification date of files
View/Arrange **I**cons/**A**utoArrange			Automatically arranges display of icons in window as you change window size
Go/**B**ack	Alt + ←	Back	Displays previously viewed window content
Go/**F**orward	Alt + →	Forward	Displays next viewed window content after using Go/Back

Matching

1. Match the following with the correct definition or function.

1) ☒   _____ **a.** restores a maximized window

2) scroll bar   _____ **b.** a mouse pointer

3) 🖥 My Computer   _____ **c.** used to see the contents of your computer

4) 📁   _____ **d.** used to provide information to complete a command

5) dialog box   _____ **e.** represents a folder

6) 📖   _____ **f.** settings associated with an object

7) properties   _____ **g.** used to bring additional information into view in a window

8) ⧉   _____ **h.** rectangular section dedicated to a specific activity or application

9) window   _____ **i.** represents a Help file

10) ⌖   _____ **j.** closes a window

2. Use the figure below to match each action with its result.

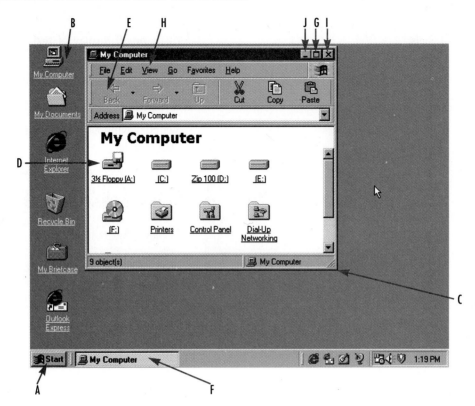

Action		Result
1) click E	_____	**a.** displays previously viewed window content
2) click G	_____	**b.** selects the A drive icon
3) click I	_____	**c.** sizes the window
4) point D	_____	**d.** minimizes the window
5) click J	_____	**e.** maximizes the window
6) click B	_____	**f.** closes the window
7) click F	_____	**g.** opens the Start menu
8) click H	_____	**h.** displays View drop-down menu
9) drag C	_____	**i.** restores a minimized window
10) click A	_____	**j.** opens the My Computer window

Fill-In Questions

1. In the following Windows 98 screen, several items are identified by letters. Enter the correct term for each item in the space provided.

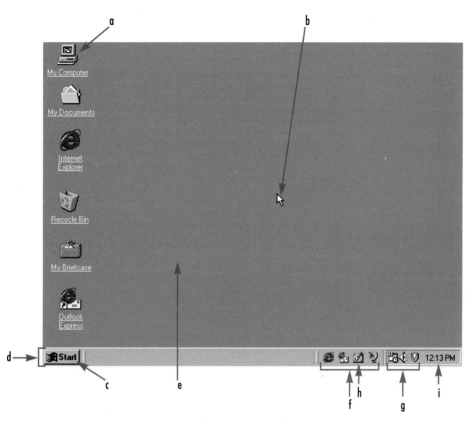

a. _____   f. _____

b. _____   g. _____

c. _____   h. _____

d. _____   i. _____

e. _____

2. In the following window, several items are identified by letters. Enter the correct term for each item in the space provided.

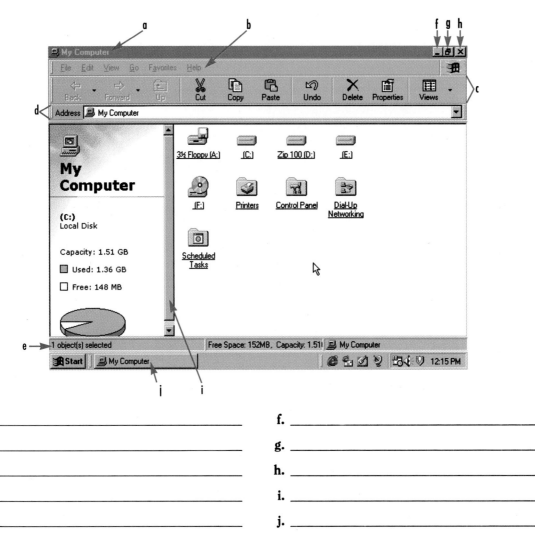

a. _____   f. _____

b. _____   g. _____

c. _____   h. _____

d. _____   i. _____

e. _____   j. _____

3. Complete the following statements by filling in the blanks with the correct terms.

a. A(n) _____ means that features you see in Windows 98 will be found in programs that run under Windows.

b. The _____ program controls computer system resources and coordinates the flow of data to input and output devices.

c. The _____ button is used to start a program, open a document, get help, find files, and change system settings.

d. Moving the mouse while holding down the left mouse button is called _____.

e. The two desktop views are _____ and _____.

f. The _____ is used with a mouse to bring additional lines of information into view.

g. When the task button appears depressed, this indicates the window is the _____ window.

h. Storing related files in _____ keeps the disk organized and makes it much easier to locate files.

i. _____ are settings and attributes associated with an object.

j. The opening Windows 98 screen is called the _____.

k. _____ divide a window into separate scrollable areas.

l. A(n) _____ scroll box indicates that only a small amount of the total available information is displayed in the window.

m. The three window arrangements are _____, _____, and _____.

n. A(n) _____ file is a file that has a specific application program associated with it.

o. Dragging the _____ of a window maintains the window proportions.

Discussion Questions

1. Windows 98 is the newest version of the Windows operating system. Using the WWW as a resource, locate the Microsoft Web site and find out what other versions of Windows operating systems are available. Write a brief report describing the different versions.

2. Different types of computers use different operating systems. OS/2, Unix, and the Macintosh operating system are others. Using the WWW as a resource, find information about each of these operating systems. Write a brief report describing the different systems.

3. While using the My Computer window, you looked at the files stored on the hard disk of your computer. Using the library or WWW as a resource, describe the construction of the hard disk and explain how a hard disk stores data.

4. The capacity or amount of data a disk can hold is measured in bytes. Using the library or WWW as a resource, define the term byte and list the most widely used floppy disks and their capacities. Using the same resources, identify the type of floppy disk with the largest capacity.

Hands-On Practice Exercises

■ ■ ■ ■ ■ ■ ■ ■ ■ ■ ■

Step by Step   Rating System   ☆ Easy
                                          ☆☆ Moderate
                                          ☆☆☆ Difficult

1. Microsoft includes with the operating system a Discover Windows 98 tutorial, which introduces and explains many of the basic Windows 98 features. This problem will use the Discover Windows 98 tutorial to reinforce many of the features presented in this lab.

Note: To use the Discover Windows 98 tutorial, you either need access to the Windows 98 CD or your school must have copied the tutorial (Discover.exe) to the hard disk of your computer or to the network.

a. Follow the instructions from your instructor to begin the Discover Windows 98 tutorial.

b. Type 1 or click on the first topic, Computer Essentials, from the contents listing to begin the tutorial.

c. Run the tutorial beginning with the first topic, Meeting Your Computer.

d. As you read and work through the tutorial, answer the following questions:

1) What part of the computer hardware is referred to as the "brain" of the computer? _____

2) What are the four main hardware components of a computer system? _____

3) What are the instructions called that tell your computer what to do? _____

4) What are the three main items displayed in the taskbar? _____

5) Explain what type of tasks and options are found in the three sections of the Start menu. _____

6) The black triangle on a menu indicates a _____ _____ or _____ _____ will be displayed.

7) What is the work area called where a program or application appears? _____ _____

8) What does the F1 function key do in most applications? _____

e. When you are done, click to exit the Discover Windows 98 tutorial.

☆☆

2. In this problem you will use Windows 98 Help to learn more about the Windows desktop and to locate information about changing the mouse properties.

a. Start Help and display the Contents tab.

b. Open the Exploring Your Computer book and then The Windows Desktop.

c. Open the topic Introducing the Windows Desktop Update. Read the Help information on this topic.

d. Open the Getting Started Book: Online Version and display the Microsoft Windows 98 Getting Started Book.

e. Notice the underlined text "Click here." This text is a shortcut link that will automatically open the feature. Click on the link to open the Getting Started manual. It appears in a second Help window. Maximize the window.

f. From the Contents tab, open the Using Your Desktop book and read the three topics.

g. Open the Exploring Your Computer book and read all topics. What Start menu option is used to open a recently opened document?

h. Open the Using a Mouse book and read all three topics. What does right-clicking an object display?

i. Close the Getting Started window.

Next you will use the Help Search tab to locate more information about using and customizing the mouse. The Search tab operates much like the Index tab.

j. Display the Search tab.

k. Enter the word "mouse" in the text box. Then click the List Topics button.

l. Display the topic "To adjust the speed of the mouse pointer."

m. Click on the "Click here" shortcut to open the Mouse Properties dialog box. Notice that this dialog box displays a [?] Help button in the title bar. Clicking this button, then clicking on an option in the dialog box will display a pop-up box of information about the feature. Look through all the tabs in the dialog box and use the [?] Help button to find out about areas or settings you may not understand. What are some of the mouse property settings and why would you want to change these settings?

n. In the Motion tab, adjust the pointer speed and turn on the Show Pointer Trails option. Move the mouse to see the results of your selections.

o. In the Buttons tab, change the double-click speed and then try out your changes by double-clicking in the test area.

p. When you are done, click [Cancel] to cancel the changes you have made and close the dialog box.

q. Close the Help window.

3. As you learned in the lab, windows can be both sized and moved. This is an important skill to develop because many times windows will cover other information you want to see or may be an inappropriate size when they are opened. To develop this skill you will open, move, and size several windows while learning about keyboard properties.

a. Open the My Computer window.

b. Open Help.

c. Display the Search tab. The Search tab operates much like the Index tab.

d. Enter the word "keyboard" in the text box. Then click the List Topics button. Display the topic "To adjust the rate at which the cursor blinks."

e. Hide the left frame of the Help window. Move the Help window to the lower right corner of the desktop.

f. Move the My Computer window to the upper left corner of the desktop.

g. Size the Help window until it covers the lower right quarter of the desktop.

h. Size the My Computer window until it covers the upper left quarter of the desktop.

i. Maximize the Help window.

j. Click on the "Click here" shortcut to open the Keyboard Properties dialog box. Notice that this dialog box displays a [?] Help button in the title bar. Clicking this button, then clicking on an option in the dialog box will display a pop-up box of information about the feature. Look through all the tabs in the dialog box and use the [?] Help button to find out about areas or settings you may not understand. What are some of the keyboard property settings and why would you want to change these settings?

k. In the Speed tab, set the repeat rate to the slowest speed and try the setting out in the Test Repeat Rate text box. Change the speed to the fastest and test it again.

l. Change the cursor blink rate setting and observe the change of the blinking cursor in the dialog box.

m. Another way to make a window active is to use the [Alt]+[Tab] "cool switch" to switch from one open window to another. When you hold down [Alt] and press [Tab], an icon road map box appears displaying icons for each open window. As you continue to hold down [Alt], you can press [Tab] to move the selection to the next icon. When you release [Alt], the window of the selected icon is the active window. Using this method, make the My Computer window active. Then use it to make the Keyboard Properties dialog box active again.

n. Restore the Help window.

o. Cascade the open windows. Undo the Cascade. What happened to the dialog box when you used cascade?

p. Click [Cancel] to cancel the keyboard property changes you made and close the dialog box.

q. Return the windows to their approximate original size.

r. Close all open windows.

4. The taskbar can be customized in many ways. In this problem you will learn about other features of the taskbar.

a. Use Help to find information about moving the taskbar, resizing it, using Auto hide, and about displaying toolbars in the taskbar.

Next follow the steps below to try out several of these features.

b. Double-click on the time in the taskbar. What happened?

c. Notice that this dialog box displays a Help button in the title bar. Clicking this button, then clicking on an option in the dialog box will display a pop-up box of information about the feature. Use the Help button for information on the Date/Time Properties dialog box. Describe the date and time properties that can be changed. Close the dialog box.

d. Select Properties from the taskbar shortcut menu. Turn on the Auto hide property. Choose OK. What happened to the taskbar?

e. To redisplay the taskbar, move the mouse pointer to the bottom of the window. Then open the Taskbar Properties dialog box and turn off the Auto hide taskbar property.

f. The taskbar can be moved along any border of the desktop. Move it to each border and describe what happens to the desktop and the taskbar. Return the taskbar to the bottom of the window.

On Your Own

5. Every item on the desktop has properties associated with it that can be changed to suit your needs. Right-click on the desktop and select Properties from the shortcut menu to open the Display Properties dialog box. Try changing several of the property settings in the Background, Screen Saver, and Appearance tabs. Describe the effects of changing properties in each tab. Use the `Cancel` button to cancel the changes you made and close the dialog box.

6. Use Help to find out about new features in Windows 98. Identify and describe five new features of the program, for example, Channels and Active Desktop.

Windows 98 Basic Skills

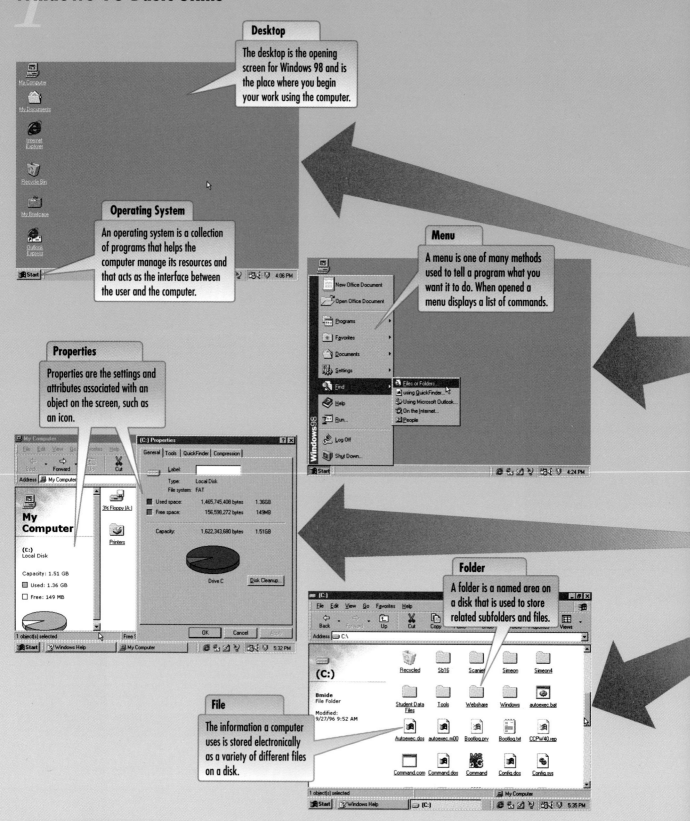

Desktop

The desktop is the opening screen for Windows 98 and is the place where you begin your work using the computer.

Operating System

An operating system is a collection of programs that helps the computer manage its resources and that acts as the interface between the user and the computer.

Menu

A menu is one of many methods used to tell a program what you want it to do. When opened a menu displays a list of commands.

Properties

Properties are the settings and attributes associated with an object on the screen, such as an icon.

Folder

A folder is a named area on a disk that is used to store related subfolders and files.

File

The information a computer uses is stored electronically as a variety of different files on a disk.

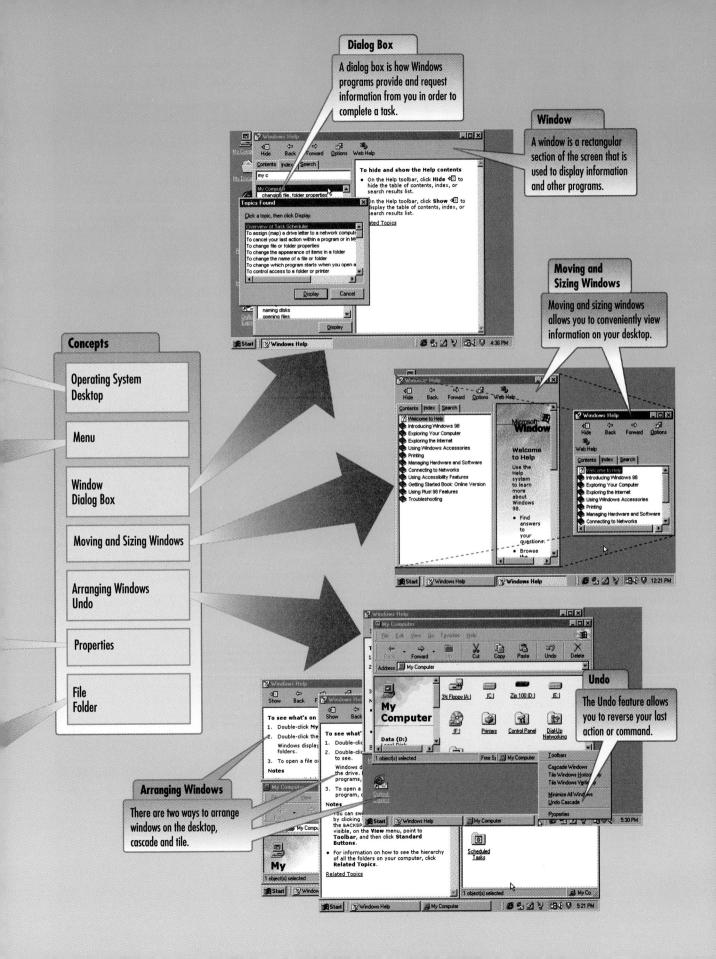

Organizing Your Work

2

COMPETENCIES

After completing this lab, you will know how to:

1. Use Explorer to manage files.
2. Copy files.
3. Use Send To.
4. Create and delete folders.
5. Delete, move, and rename files.
6. Extend a selection.
7. Find files.
8. Use WordPad.
9. Open and edit a document.
10. Format text.
11. Save a file.
12. Preview and print a document.
13. Create a shortcut icon.
14. Print a window.
15. Use the Recycle Bin.

Organizational skills are very important skills in any profession. When you are disorganized, it takes much longer to complete tasks accurately. In this lab you will learn to use Windows Explorer to organize the folders and files on your disk. You will learn how to create folders and copy and move files into folders to make it easy to quickly locate files. Additionally, you will learn about many other file management features and shortcuts that will improve your efficiency.

The primary use of a computer is to run software application programs to complete a task such as creating a letter or a financial report. In this lab you will also learn how to use a simple word processor program, WordPad, that is included with Windows 98. The features you will use to create, edit, format, and print a document are features that are common to all applications that run under Windows. Learning about many of these features now will make it easier for you to learn to use new applications in the future. The document you will edit is shown here.

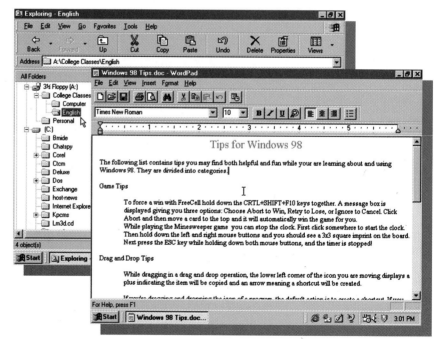

Concept Overview

The following concepts will be introduced in this lab:

1. Hierarchy
The graphic representation of the organization of folders on a disk is called a hierarchy.

2. Copy and Move
All Windows applications include features that allow you to copy and move selected information from one location to another.

3. File and Folder Names
When a file or folder is created, it must be assigned a file name that identifies its contents.

4. Drag and Drop
Common to all Windows applications is the ability to copy or move selections using the drag and drop feature.

5. Word Processor
Word processing application programs are designed to help you create, edit, and print text documents.

6. Saving Files
When you save a document you are working on, a permanent copy of your onscreen document is electronically stored as a file on a disk.

7. Shortcut Icon
Shortcut icons immediately open their associated item, making them a powerful tool for increasing efficiency.

Part 1

Using Explorer

Windows 98 includes the Explorer program, whose primary purpose is to help you navigate through and organize the folders and files on a disk. Although similar in purpose to My Computer, it provides a more efficient and powerful means of browsing that makes it easier to view and organize the information on your disk.

You can start the Windows Explorer program as you do most programs, by choosing it from the Programs menu of the Start menu. However, it is quicker to choose the command from the My Computer shortcut menu.

■   Turn on the computer. If necessary, close the Welcome window.

To display the shortcut menu, right-click on 🖳 .
My Computer

■   Display the My Computer shortcut menu.

■   Choose **E**xplore.

■   Maximize the Exploring window.

> The Exploring window on your screen may display different folders and icons than those in Figure 2-1.

Your screen should be similar to Figure 2-1.

the All Folders Explorer Bar displays the contents of your disk as a hierarchy

selected folder

the contents frame displays the contents of the selected folder

FIGURE 2-1

main folder

subfolders under My Computer folder

Desktop icons appear under Desktop main folder

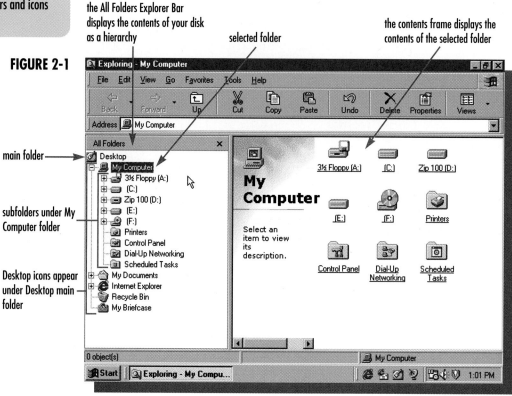

Like the My Computer window, the Exploring window includes a menu bar, the Standard Buttons toolbar, the Address Bar, and a status bar. The menu bar contains the same menus as in My Computer, with the addition of the Tools menu. As in My Computer, you can change the display of icons and the window view.

- If necessary, make the following adjustments to the Exploring window using the View menu.

    - Display the Standard Buttons toolbar with text labels.

    - Display the Address Bar toolbar.

    - Display the status bar.

    - Change the view to Large Icons.

    - Set the view to display in Web view (View/as Web Page).

> You can adjust the size of the frames by dragging the bar that separates the two frames.

The left side of the Exploring window displays the All Folders Explorer Bar. **Explorer Bars** provide a means for you to browse a list of items while the contents of the selected item are displayed on the right side of the window. The All Folders Explorer Bar is used to browse the contents of a disk. It displays the information about your computer's disk drive as a hierarchy.

Concept 1: Hierarchy

The graphic representation of the organization of folders on a disk is called a **hierarchy.** The top-level folder of a disk is the **main folder.** On the hard disk, the main folder is represented by the Desktop icon (see Figure 2-2). On a floppy disk, the main folder is generally represented by the drive icon. The main folder always appears at the top of the hierarchy. Folders created in the main folder appear indented below the main folder and are visually connected by the leftmost vertical line. **Subfolders** appear indented below other folders and are connected by another vertical line. Because of the branching nature of the hierarchy, it is sometimes also called a **tree.**

The folders that appear indented and connected by a vertical line under the Desktop icon are the same as the icons that represent these folders on the desktop. The folders under the My Computer folder are subfolders. They appear indented below the My Computer folder and are connected vertically by a line.

The right side of the window is the same as the My Computer window. It displays the contents of the selected folder in the All Folders bar. In this case, because you started Windows Explorer from the My Computer shortcut menu, the My Computer folder is selected, indicating it is open. The contents frame shows icons for the drives on your computer and the same folders as you saw in the My Computer window.

Choosing a different item in the All Folders bar opens the item and displays the contents of the item in the contents frame. To see the contents of the hard drive,

■   Click 💾 (C:) (or the appropriate drive for your system).

Your screen should be similar to Figure 2-2.

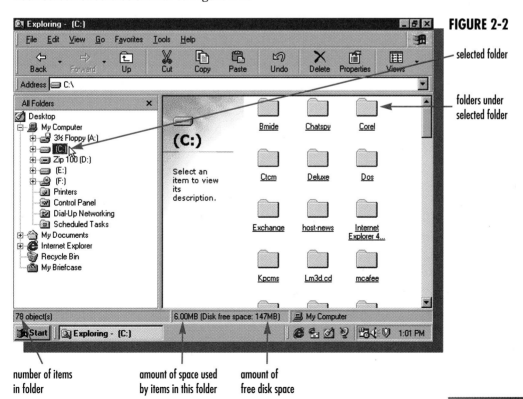

FIGURE 2-2

selected folder

folders under selected folder

number of items in folder

amount of space used by items in this folder

amount of free disk space

The contents frame on your screen will reflect the folders and files on your computer's hard drive.

The ⊞ appears only if the object contains folders or subfolders.

The contents frame displays the contents of the selected item. If the selected item contains folders, they are displayed first, in alphabetical order, followed by the files. The status bar displays information about the number of objects and the disk properties of the selected item.

You can also display the folders in the All Folders bar. To do this you click the ⊞ sign that is displayed to the left of the drive icon. This expands the hierarchy. To display the folders on your hard drive,

■ Click ⊞ to the left of the hard drive icon (C:).

Your screen should be similar to Figure 2-3.

FIGURE 2-3

indicates folder is expanded and displays all subfolders

third branch of hierarchy

indicates folder contains subfolders

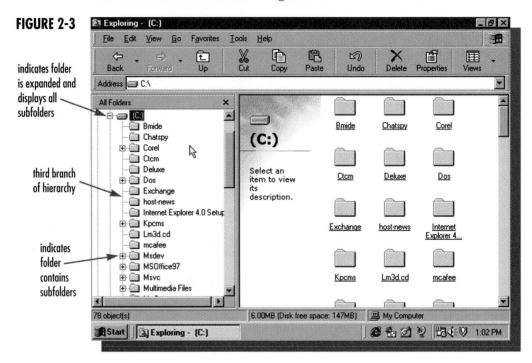

The All Folders bar displays the folders on your hard drive as a third branch on the hierarchy. Notice that the ⊞ changed to a ⊟, which shows that the drive icon is fully open or expanded. You can also expand a folder that contains subfolders.

■ If necessary, scroll the All Folders bar to see the Program Files folder icon.

■ Expand the Programs Files folder.

The folders in the Program Files folder appear as a fourth branch on the hierarchy. Notice, however, that the contents frame still displays the contents of the C drive. This is because the Program Files folder is not yet selected. To see the contents of this folder,

■ Click the Program Files folder name.

The folder name is highlighted, and the folder icon appears as 🗁, indicating the folder is open. When a folder is open, it is the **current folder** or the folder that will be affected by your next actions. The contents of the current folder are displayed in the contents frame, and the name of the current folder appears at the top of the contents area.

■ Click on the Accessories folder name.

Your screen should be similar to Figure 2-4.

FIGURE 2-4

Now the Accessories folder is current, and the contents are displayed in the contents frame, but the folder is not expanded in the hierarchy. Notice that the Address Bar displays the **path** or chain of folder names that specifies the location of the current folder on the disk. The drive name (in this case C:) is always displayed at the beginning of the path. The folder names follow the drive and are separated by \.

To hide or collapse the display of the Program Files folders again in the All Folders frame,

■ Click ⊟ to the left of the Program Files folder icon.

> If you double-click on a closed folder, it will both expand it and open it.

> You can also double-click on an open folder to expand or hide the folders in the All Folders frame.

Copying Files

One of the major purposes for using Windows Explorer is to help you manage the files on your computer. This commonly involves copying and moving files to other locations, either on the same disk or to another disk.

Concept 2: Copy and Move

All Windows applications include features that allow you to copy and move selected items from one location to another. When an item is copied, the item remains in the original location, and a duplicate is created in the new location. When an item is moved, it is deleted from the original location, and a duplicate is created in the new location.

The process of copying and moving requires the use of three commands, Cut, Copy, and Paste, located on the Edit menu. Toolbar shortcuts for these commands are also found on the Standard toolbars of most applications. The item to be copied or moved must first be selected by highlighting it. The location that contains the information you want to cut or copy is called the **source.** Then, choose Copy to create a copy of the selection or Cut to move a selection. In both cases a duplicate of the selection is copied to a temporary storage area in memory called the **Clipboard.** Next you select the location, called the **destination,** where you want the copy of the information that is stored in the Clipboard to appear. Finally you use the Paste command to actually insert the item in the new location.

Now that you know how to browse your computer to locate folders and files, you will copy the files needed to complete this lab (and others your instructor may be using) to your data disk. Before a disk can be used, it must be **formatted.** This prepares a disk to accept information and files. Most disks are sold preformatted and can be used immediately. However, if your disk is not already formatted, refer to Appendix A for procedures on formatting before continuing.

■   Insert your data disk in drive A.

The files you will copy should be in a folder on your hard disk. First you need to open the folder containing the data files.

■   Locate and expand the Student Data Files folder.

■   Open the Windows 98 folder.

Next, you will copy the file named Class Schedule.txt to your data disk. To specify which file you want to copy, you must first select it by highlighting it.

■   Point to Class Schedule.txt.

This text assumes drive A is the drive you will use for your data disk. If your system is different, select the appropriate drive for your system in place of A throughout this lab.

This text assumes the files are in a folder named Student Data Files on your hard drive. If your school uses a different folder name, or your computer is on a network and the data files are in a folder on another system disk, your instructor will provide additional instructions.

Your screen should be similar to Figure 2-5.

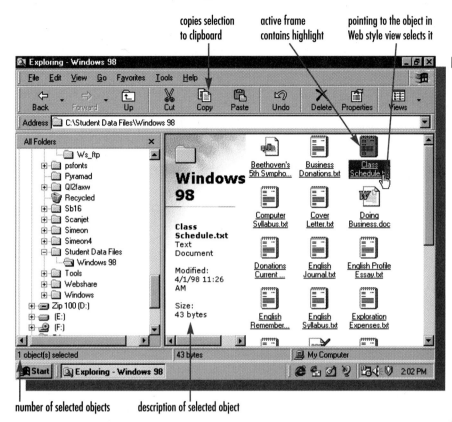

FIGURE 2-5

copies selection to clipboard · active frame contains highlight · pointing to the object in Web style view selects it

number of selected objects · description of selected object

The Class Schedule.txt icon is highlighted, indicating it is selected. The right frame containing the highlight is the **active frame,** or the frame that will be affected by the next action you perform. To copy the file,

■ Click 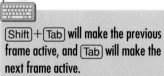.

When you use the Copy command, a copy of the selected item, in this case the file, is stored in the Clipboard. Now you need to tell Windows 98 where you want the file copied to by specifying the destination. Your destination will be the disk in the floppy drive. To select the destination, you need to make the All Folders bar active and make the drive containing your data disk current.

■ Click 3½ Floppy (A:) in the All Folders bar.

The contents frame does not display any icons because there are no files or folders on this disk yet. The Paste command is used to insert the copy of the information, which is stored in the Clipboard, to the selected destination.

■ Click Paste.

Shift + Tab will make the previous frame active, and Tab will make the next frame active.

The menu equivalent is **E**dit/**C**opy, and the shortcut key is Ctrl + C. Copy is also on the selected object's shortcut menu.

You may need to scroll the All Folders bar to see the floppy drive icon.

You can also use the **E**dit/**P**aste command, the shortcut key Ctrl + V, or **P**aste on the Exploring Window shortcut menu.

A Copying message box is briefly displayed as the file is copied. This box shows the progress of the copy procedure and indicates the amount of time remaining until the procedure is complete.

Your screen should be similar to Figure 2-6.

FIGURE 2-6

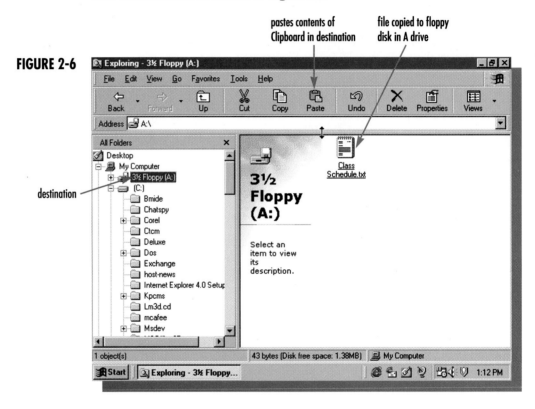

The contents frame is updated, and the Class Schedule file icon is displayed. The file was copied to the main folder of the floppy disk (this folder was created when the disk was formatted). You are now ready to copy the rest of the files to your data disk.

■ Make the Windows 98 folder current again.

Notice that the Class Schedule file is still displayed in the Windows 98 contents area. Because you copied the file, it is now in both the Windows 98 folder and on your data disk.

Using Send To

Next you need to copy the other Windows 98 data files to the main folder of your data disk. Instead of using Copy and Paste, you can use the Send To command on the File menu. This command makes the process easier by allowing you to copy files directly to the main folder of a destination disk without having to select it first.

Rather than select and copy each file individually, you will select all the files in the folder and copy them at the same time.

■   Choose <u>E</u>dit/Select <u>A</u>ll.

All the file icons in the current folder are selected. To quickly copy the files to the disk in the floppy drive,

■   Choose <u>F</u>ile/Send <u>T</u>o.

Your screen should be similar to Figure 2-7.

The shortcut for this command is
Ctrl + A.

The Send To command is also on the selected object's shortcut menu.

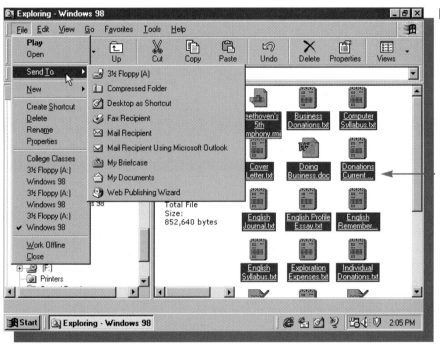

FIGURE 2-7

all files selected

The Send To submenu lists the locations to which you can copy the files. To select the drive where you want the copied files sent,

■   Click 3½ Floppy (A:) .

The Copying message box is displayed as the files are copied. In addition, because the Class Schedule file is already on the disk in drive A, a Confirm File Replace dialog box appears.

Your screen should be similar to Figure 2-8.

FIGURE 2-8

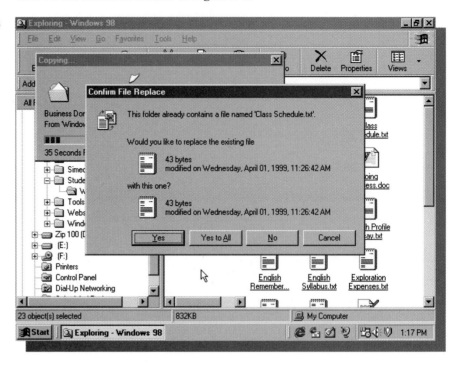

Windows 98 displays this message to prevent you from accidentally writing over a file with another that has the same name. The dialog box shows the size of the duplicate files and date and time the files were last modified. Because you just copied the Class Schedule file, you can overwrite it without changing its contents, or you can choose No to bypass this operation and continue. To bypass copying this file again,

■ Click [No].

There are no other duplicate files, and all the remaining files are copied to the main folder of your data disk.

To view the contents of your data disk, you could select the drive icon from the All Folders frame as you did previously. However, when the disk contains a large number of folders, this requires scrolling the frame. A quicker way to change locations is to select the location from the Address Bar drop-down list.

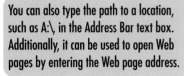

You can also type the path to a location, such as A:\, in the Address Bar text box. Additionally, it can be used to open Web pages by entering the Web page address.

■ Click [▼] at the right end of the Address Bar to display the drop-down list.

A brief version of the disk hierarchy is displayed. To switch to the drive containing your data disk,

■ Click 🖫 3½ Floppy (A:)

The contents area displays the files that were copied to your data disk.

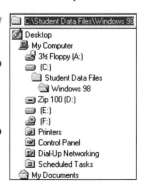

Creating Folders

Now that you have learned how Windows organizes folders and files, you will learn how to create folders to organize the files on your disk. As you add more files to the main folder of a disk, it gets very crowded and disorganized. This is especially true of hard disks, which can hold large amounts of data. To help organize files into like categories, you can create folders. For example, you may want to store software programs and the files you create using these programs by the program type. Alternatively, you might want to store your programs and information by project. You can create further divisions within each folder by creating additional subfolders.

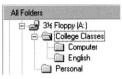

Currently the files on your data disk are simply alphabetically arranged by name in the main folder. You will create folders for the related files to help organize your disk. The folders and subfolder hierarchy you will create is shown here.

The first folder you will create on your data disk will be used to hold school-related documents. The command to create a folder is New on the File menu. To indicate where you want the folder created, the destination location must be open first. Since the drive containing your data disk is already open, you are ready to create the folder.

■ Choose <u>F</u>ile/<u>N</u>ew/<u>F</u>older.

Your screen should be similar to Figure 2-9.

FIGURE 2-9

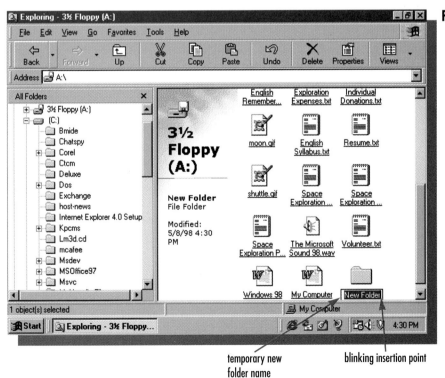

temporary new folder name

blinking insertion point

A New Folder icon is displayed in the contents frame. The temporary folder name is highlighted, and the insertion point is displayed at the end of the folder name. This indicates that Windows 98 is waiting for you to replace the default name with a descriptive name for the folder you are creating.

Concept 3: File and Folder Names

When a file or folder is created, it must be assigned a **file name** that identifies its contents. The name you assign a file must be unique for the folder it is in. For example, if you give a new file the same name as an existing file in the same folder, the contents of the original file will be replaced by the contents of the new file. Folder names must also be unique.

In addition to a file name, a **file name extension** may be added. A file name extension is up to three characters and is separated from the file name by a period. Generally a file name extension is used to identify the type of file. It is not always necessary to enter a file name extension, because most application programs automatically add an identifying file name extension to any files created using the program. For instance, a file created using Microsoft Word has a file name extension of "doc." A folder extension is not generally used and is never supplied by the operating system.

The parts of a file name are shown below.

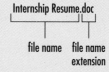

file name   file name extension

Windows 98 and programs that are designed to operate under Windows 98 allow you to use long folder and file names of up to 255 characters. They can contain the letters A to Z, the numbers 0 to 9, and any of the following special characters: underscore (_), caret (^), dollar sign ($), tilde (~), exclamation point (!), number sign (#), percent sign (%), ampersand (&), hyphen (-), braces ({}), parentheses (), "at" sign (@), apostrophe ('), and the grave accent (`). Spaces are allowed in names, but the following characters are not allowed: \ / : * ? " < > |.

> The restrictions regarding characters also apply to file name extensions.

Because this folder will be used to hold files related to your school work, you will name the new folder College Classes. With the text "New Folder" highlighted,

■ Type **College Classes**

■ Press ⏎Enter.

The folder name appears exactly as you typed it (including case). The insertion point is no longer displayed, but the folder is still selected.

Next you want to create another folder under the main folder to hold your personal files. Although the College Classes folder is the selected folder, the main folder is still current.

> If you make a typing error, use the ⬅Backspace key to delete the characters to the left of the insertion point.

■   Create a new folder named Personal.

The Personal folder is displayed in the contents frame. Now that the disk in the drive contains folders, the drive icon in the All Folders bar is preceded with a ⊞.

■   Expand the A floppy drive icon to display the folders in the All Folders bar.

Your screen should be similar to Figure 2-10.

main folder of disk
in A drive

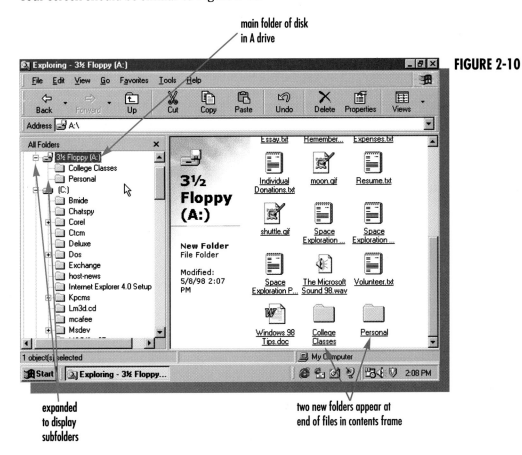

FIGURE 2-10

expanded
to display
subfolders

two new folders appear at
end of files in contents frame

The two folders you created appear in alphabetical order in the All Folders area. However, the two new folders are not yet displayed in alphabetical order in the contents frame. To update the order of display of icons in the contents frame,

■   Choose View/Arrange Icons/by Name.

The folders now appear first in the contents frame and in alphabetical order.

Next you would like to further subdivide your files in the College Classes folder by classes: Computer and English. To create a subfolder under the College Classes folder, you must first make the College Classes folder current.

■   Open the College Classes folder in the All Folders bar.

■   Create a folder named English.

The new folder is displayed in the College Classes contents frame, and a ⊞ appears next to the College Classes folder in the All Folders bar to show that the folder contains a subfolder.

- ■ Next create the Computer subfolder in the College Classes folder. (Make sure the College Classes folder is current first.)

- ■ Arrange the folders alphabetically by name.

- ■ Then, to display the folders in the All Folders bar, expand the College Classes folder.

Your screen should be similar to Figure 2-11.

new folders arranged
alphabetically by name

FIGURE 2-11

subfolders in
College Classes folder

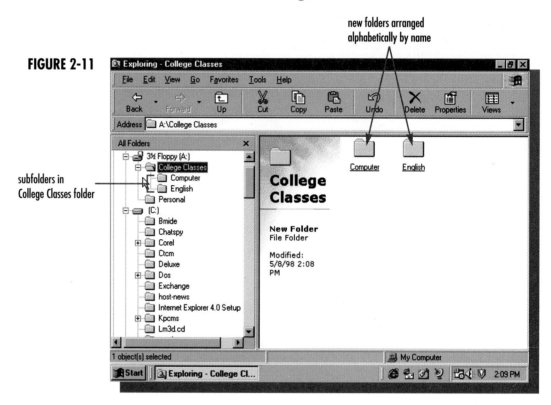

Copying a File to a Folder

Next you will copy the file Class Schedule.txt from the main folder of your data disk into the College Classes folder.

- ■ Make the A drive current.

- ■ Select the Class Schedule.txt file icon in the contents frame.

If you accidentally clicked on the file icon, it will open the file in a separate window. Close the window and then point to the file icon to select it.

Another way to copy or move a file is to use the drag and drop feature.

Concept 4: Drag and Drop

Common to all Windows applications is the ability to copy or move selections using the **drag and drop** feature. After selecting the item to be copied or moved, pointing to it and dragging the mouse moves or copies the selection to the new location specified when you release the mouse button. The location you want to drag and drop to should be visible in the window.

If you drag a file to a folder on the same disk, it will be moved. If you drag a file to a folder on another disk, it will be copied. You can hold down (Shift) while dragging to always move a file, or (Ctrl) to copy a file. If you drag holding down the right mouse button, a shortcut menu appears with options to either copy or move the selection.

You will drag and drop the selected file icon from the contents frame to the College Classes folder in the All Folders bar.

■ With the mouse pointer on the selected file icon, hold down (Ctrl) and drag to the College Classes folder in the All Folders bar.

■ When the pointer is positioned over the College Classes folder and the folder is selected, release the mouse button and (Ctrl).

■ Make the College Classes folder current.

Your screen should be similar to Figure 2-12.

The mouse pointer appears as ⬚ while copying a file using drag and drop.

A circle/slash symbol ⊘ is displayed when the mouse pointer is in an area where the file cannot be copied or moved.

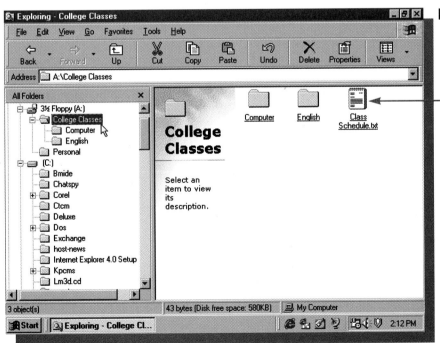

FIGURE 2-12

file copied from main folder to College Classes folder

The contents frame displays a file icon for the copied file.

Deleting Files

At some point, some of the files you have on your disk may no longer be needed and you will want to remove them from your disk to save space. You will delete the Class Schedule file from the main folder now that you have a copy of it in the College Classes folder. When the folder you want to move to is above the current folder, you can quickly move up one level at a time in the hierarchy using the [🔼 Up] button. To move up one level to the main folder and delete this file,

The menu equivalent is <u>G</u>o/<u>U</u>p One Level.

You can also use the Delete command on the File or shortcut menu or the shortcut key [Delete] to delete a selected object.

■ Click [🔼 Up].

■ Select the Class Schedule.txt file icon in the contents frame.

■ Click [✕ Delete].

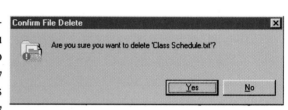

The Confirm File Delete message box appears in which you must confirm that you want to remove the file. This is especially important when deleting files from a floppy disk, because they are permanently deleted. Files and folders that are deleted from the hard disk are not permanently deleted, but are placed in the Recycle Bin where they are held until they are permanently deleted from that location. If you changed your mind, choosing [No] would cancel the procedure. To continue,

You will learn more about the Recycle Bin later in this lab.

You cannot use Undo to reverse the action of deleting a file from a floppy disk.

■ Click [Yes].

Your screen should be similar to Figure 2-13.

FIGURE 2-13

deletes selected object

blank space left
after object deleted

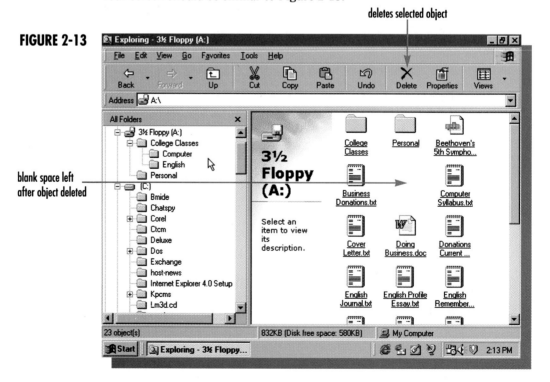

The file is removed from the main folder of the disk, and its icon is no longer displayed in the contents frame.

Moving Files

Rather than copying and deleting files, you can move them from one location to another. You would like to move the file English Syllabus to the College Classes folder.

- Select the English Syllabus file icon from the main folder of your data disk.

- Drag the English Syllabus file icon to the College Classes folder in the All Folders bar.

When the move is complete, the English Syllabus file icon is no longer displayed in the contents frame.

- To see the file icon in the College Classes folder, make the College Classes folder current.

The English Syllabus file icon is displayed in the folder. However, you decide you want this file to be in one of the subfolders of the College Classes folder. It should really be in the English folder. To undo the move,

- Click [Undo] .

The move is reversed, and the English Syllabus file is removed from the College Classes folder and placed back in the main folder.

- Make the main folder current again and move the English Syllabus file to the English folder.

- Open the English folder to verify that the file was moved to the correct location.

Extending a Selection

You can also select several files to copy or move at the same time. This is called **extending a selection.** You can quickly select several files that are scattered throughout the list by holding down [Ctrl] while pointing to the file icons. First you will move two nonadjacent files, Cover Letter.txt and Resume.txt, to the Personal folder.

- Make the main folder of your data disk current.

- Select the Cover Letter.txt file icon.

- If necessary, scroll the window to see the Resume file.

- Hold down [Ctrl].

- Select the Resume file icon.

- If necessary, deselect any other files that you may have selected accidentally.

- Release [Ctrl].

> You can also use the Cut and Paste commands on the Edit or shortcut menu or the toolbar buttons [Cut] and [Paste] to move a file.

> The menu equivalent is **E**dit/**U**ndo, and the keyboard shortcut is [Ctrl]+Z. The action that will be undone appears after the command name in the menu.

> You can also move a file to a folder displayed in the contents frame.

> Reminder: You can click [Up] to move up a level.

> To deselect a file (remove the highlight), point to it again while holding down [Ctrl].

Your screen should be similar to Figure 2-14.

FIGURE 2-14

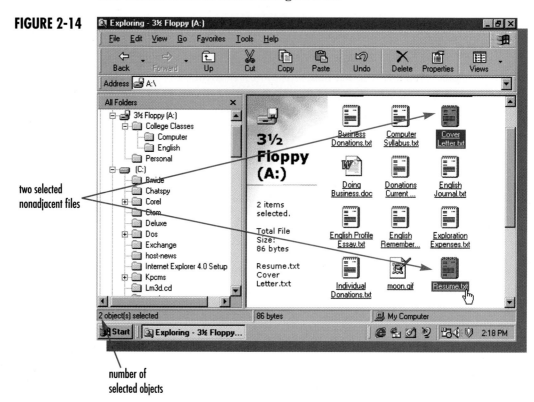

two selected
nonadjacent files

number of
selected objects

The two files are highlighted, and the status bar indicates that two objects are selected.

■ Move the files to the Personal folder.

■ To verify that the files were moved, open the Personal folder.

Next you will move a series of adjacent files from the main folder to the English folder of the College Classes folder.

■ Make the main folder of your data disk current.

You will select the three adjacent files, English Journal, English Profile Essay, and English Remembered Person Essay. To do this simply hold down the mouse button and drag to create a box around the files. If a file you do not want selected is included in the box, hold down Ctrl while pointing to the file to deselect it, leaving all others selected. Likewise, you can add other files to the selection by holding down Ctrl while selecting them.

■ Select the English Journal, English Profile Essay, and English Remembered Person Essay files by dragging a box around the file icons and adding or clearing selections as needed.

■ Move the selected files to the English folder under the College Classes folder.

■ To verify that the files were moved, open the English folder.

> You can also use drag and drop with multiple files.

> A Moving message box appears when multiple files are moved.

Your screen should be similar to Figure 2-15.

three selected files
moved to English folder

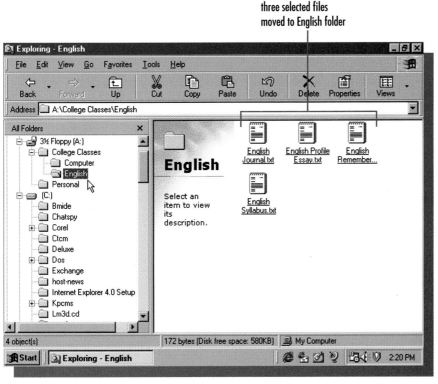

FIGURE 2-15

The file icons for the files you moved are displayed in the contents area.

Renaming Files

Next you want to change the name of the Class Schedule file in the College Classes folder. This file actually contains the class schedules for the Fall semester only. You will rename this file Fall Class Schedule so that it is more descriptive of the information it contains.

- ■ Open the College Classes folder.
- ■ Right-click on the Class Schedule icon to display the shortcut menu.
- ■ Choose Rena<u>m</u>e.

The file name appears highlighted and with an insertion point, just as a new folder name appears. To move the insertion point to the beginning of the file name and add the word "Fall" to the file name,

> You can also use the Rena<u>m</u>e command on the <u>F</u>ile menu.

- ■ Press Ctrl + Home.
- ■ Type **Fall**
- ■ Press Spacebar.
- ■ Press ←Enter.

The file name changes to its new name, Fall Class Schedule.

Deleting Folders

At some point, some of the folders you have on your disk may no longer be needed and you will want to remove them from your disk. As you learned earlier, to delete a file you select it, then use the Delete command to remove it. The same procedure is used to delete folders. In addition, when a folder is selected, using Delete will also remove all the files and subfolders contained within that folder. You will use the keyboard shortcut to delete the folder.

■ Make the Personal folder current.

■ Press [Delete].

The Confirm Folder Delete message box is displayed, asking you to confirm that you want to delete the folder and its contents. If you select [No], the deletion procedure is canceled. To continue,

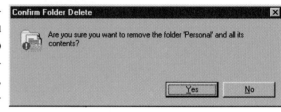

■ Click [Yes].

The Personal folder and all the files within it are removed. The All Folders bar now only displays the College Classes folder and subfolders.

Finding Files

As you add more and more files to your disk, you may have trouble remembering what folder you stored a file in or what you named it. Windows 98 has a Find Files and Folders option that can help you locate files or folders. You will use this feature to find the file English Syllabus.

> You can also use Find in the Start menu to access this feature.

■ Choose Tools/Find/Files or Folders.

The Find: All Files dialog box on your screen should be similar to Figure 2-16.

FIGURE 2-16

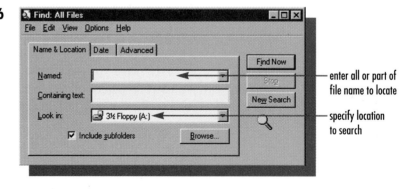

enter all or part of file name to locate

specify location to search

This dialog box allows you to find files and folders by name, by text contained in the document, or by date last modified and file size. When searching by name, you can enter the entire file name or any part of it. The more precise the information you provide, the closer the matches that are found. To locate the English Syllabus file,

- Type **english**

- If necessary, from the Look In drop down list, select the A drive.

- Click [Find Now] .

The Find dialog box on your screen should be similar to Figure 2-17.

> The Find feature is not case sensitive.

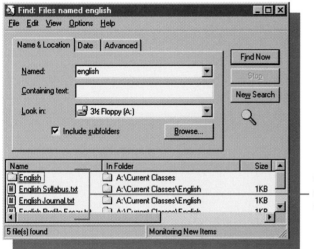

FIGURE 2-17

all files and folders in specified location containing the word "English"

The dialog box now displays all the files and folders on your data disk that contain the word "English." Using this feature makes finding files quick and easy.

- Close the Find dialog box.

- Close the Exploring window.

> Clicking on a file or folder in the Find dialog box will open it in a separate window.

Note: If you are ending your lab session now, quit Windows 98.

Part 2

Using WordPad

The primary activity a computer is used for is to run application programs to accomplish various tasks, such as creating a letter or a picture. In addition to the programs that run as part of Windows 98, such as Windows Explorer, Windows 98 includes several small programs that are designed to help you with your work, or amuse you while passing time. Some, but not all, are installed automatically on the hard disk of the computer when Windows 98 is installed. Others must be added individually. The table below lists and briefly describes many of these programs.

Application	Description
Active Movie Control	Plays audio and video files.
My Briefcase	Helps keep the various copies of your files updated by quickly transferring files between a laptop and desktop computer.
Backup	Creates backup files of files on your hard disk.
CD Player	Plays music from CDs using the CD disk drive.
Calculator	Performs simple as well as advanced scientific and statistical calculations.
Character Map	Inserts symbols/characters in documents.
Clipboard Viewer	Displays contents of Windows Clipboard.
Compression Agent	Compresses selected files to save disk space.
Dial-Up Networking	Connects to another computer or to your corporate network by using a modem.
Direct Cable Connection	Gains access to shared folders on another computer, even when your computer is not on a network. If the other computer is connected to a network, you can also gain access to that network.
Disk Cleanup	Frees up space on your hard drive to find temporary files, Internet cache files, and unnecessary program files that you can safely delete.
Disk Defragmenter	Rearranges files and unused space on your hard disk so that programs run faster.
Drive Converter	Converts your drive to the FAT32 file system, allowing your system to store data more efficiently, load programs faster, and use fewer system resources.
DriveSpace 3	Compresses files on both hard and floppy disks to create more free space for files.
Games	Solitaire, Minesweeper, Hearts, and Free Cell.
HyperTerminal	Connects via modem to a remote computer, sends/receives files, connects to computer bulletin boards and other information programs.
Kodak Imaging	Allows you to view, annotate, and perform basic tasks with image documents, including fax documents and scanned images.
Maintenance Wizard	Makes your programs run faster, checks your hard disk for problems, and frees up hard disk space.
Media Player	Plays audio, video, and animation files.
Mouse Pointers	Variety of easy-to-see pointers.
Net Watcher	Allows you to see who is currently using resources on your computer. Adds shared folders and disconnects users from your computer or from specific files.
Notepad	Used to create or edit text files that do not require formatting and are smaller than 64K.
Paint	Used to create, modify, or view pictures. You can paste a Paint picture into another document you have created, or use it as your desktop background. You can even use Paint to view and edit scanned photos.

Application	Description
Phone Dialer	Dials phone numbers in your personal phone book using your modem or another Windows telephony device.
Quick View	Previews document without opening it.
Resource Meter	Monitors the system resources your programs are using.
ScanDisk	Checks your hard disk for logical and physical errors and can then repair the damaged areas.
Scheduled Tasks	Used to schedule a task (such as Disk Defragmenter) to run when it is most convenient for you.
Screen Savers	Displays moving images when computer is idle.
Sound Recorder	Records and plays sounds.
System Monitor	Tracks the performance of your computer or your network.
System File Checker	Verifies the integrity of your operating system files, to restore them if they are corrupted, and to extract compressed files (such as drivers) from your installation disks.
System Information	Collects your system configuration information and provides a menu for displaying the associated system topics.
Welcome to Windows 98	Introduction to Windows 98 new programs and features.
WordPad	Word processor for short memos and documents.

One of the most useful programs supplied with Windows 98 is the word processing program, WordPad.

Concept 5: Word Processor

Word processing application programs are designed to help you create, edit, and print text documents. Text documents consist of all forms of written materials, such as memos, letters, brochures, newsletters, and research papers. Word processors have replaced the typewriter, and moreover have greatly enhanced what a typewriter could do. The biggest advantage of a word processor is that it displays the text as you type it on your computer screen rather than on paper. This makes it easy to make changes and corrections onscreen before the document is printed. Word processors are probably the most used of all application programs and are credited with producing the highest gains in user productivity.

One of the files supplied on your data disk is a word processing document of tips for using Windows 98. You will view, modify, and print this document using WordPad.

■ Choose **Start**/Programs/
Accessories/WordPad.

■ If necessary, maximize the window.

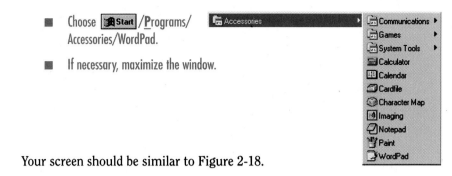

Your screen should be similar to Figure 2-18.

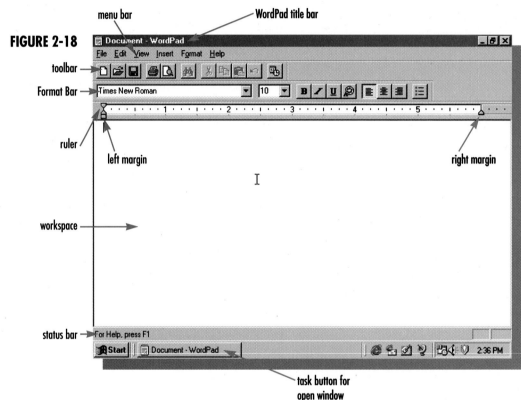

FIGURE 2-18

The WordPad application program is opened in its own window, and the taskbar displays a button for the open application. As in the other Windows 98 programs you have used, the WordPad window displays a title bar, menu bar, and toolbars. The upper toolbar contains buttons that are used to complete the most frequently used menu commands. The bottom is the Format Bar. It contains buttons that are used to enhance the appearance of the document. Additionally, as in most word processing applications, a **ruler** is displayed that shows the left and right margin settings and the line length in inches. The large blank area below the ruler is the **workspace** where your work is displayed.

■ If any of the WordPad window features shown in Figure 2-18 are not displayed on your screen, use the View menu to select the appropriate option to turn on the feature.

Opening a File

When WordPad first opens, a blank workspace is ready for you to begin typing to create a new document. Alternatively, as you will do, you can open and then modify an existing document. As in all Windows applications, the Open command on the File menu is used to open files. In addition, the toolbar shortcut 🖿 Open can be used instead of the menu command.

- Insert your data disk in the A floppy disk drive (or the appropriate drive for your system).
- Click 🖿 Open.

The menu equivalent is **File/Open**, and the keyboard shortcut is Ctrl + **O**.

The Open dialog box on your screen should be similar to Figure 2-19.

specifies location to find document to open

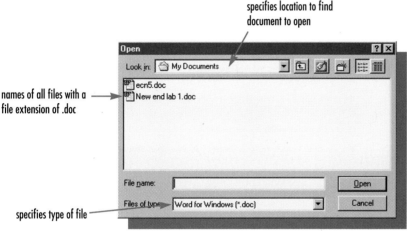

names of all files with a file extension of .doc

specifies type of file

FIGURE 2-19

This dialog box is used to specify the location and name of the file you want to open. The Look In drop-down list box displays the default location where files are saved on your computer system. You need to change this location to the drive containing your data disk.

- Open the Look In drop-down list.
- Select 💾 3½ Floppy (A:) (or the drive containing your data disk).

The large list box displays the names of all Word files on your data disk. Only Word document files (with a file extension of .doc) are displayed because the Files of Type list box shows that the currently selected type is Word documents.

- Select Windows 98 Tips.doc.
- Click 🔲 Open .

If necessary, scroll the list box until the file name Windows 98 Tips is visible. If the file name is not displayed, ask your instructor for help.

You can also double-click the file name to both select and open it.

Your screen should be similar to Figure 2-20.

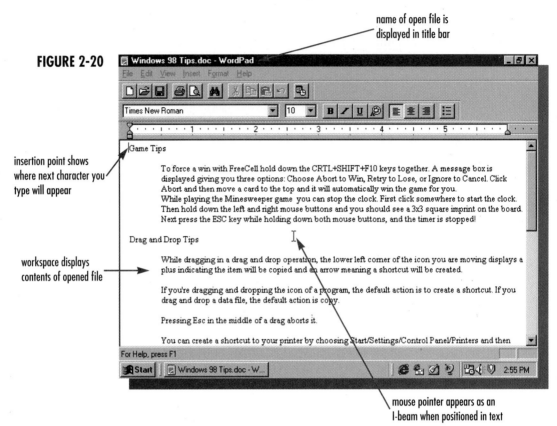

FIGURE 2-20

name of open file is displayed in title bar

insertion point shows where next character you type will appear

workspace displays contents of opened file

mouse pointer appears as an I-beam when positioned in text

The file is loaded and displayed in the workspace, and the file name is displayed in the title bar before the program name. The insertion point in the upper left corner of the document shows where the next character will appear when you begin to type. When the mouse pointer is positioned in the workspace, it appears as an I-beam, just as it does in a text box of a dialog box, and is used to position the insertion point in the document.

Editing a Document

While typing, you will certainly make typing errors or you will want to change what you have typed. One of the advantages of using a computer is that you can easily change or **edit** your documents. The changes you make can be as simple as correcting the spelling of a word or adding or removing some text, or as complicated as rearranging the content and redesigning the layout of the document.

The first change you want to make to this document is to add a title and an introductory paragraph. As you are typing, the insertion point moves to show you where the next character will appear. Do not be concerned if you make a mistake, as you will learn about correcting errors next.

■   Type **Tips for Windows 98**

■   Press ⬅Enter twice.

Pressing ⏎Enter ends a line and moves the insertion point to the beginning of the next line. When the insertion point is at the beginning of a line and ⏎Enter is pressed, a blank line is created. To continue, enter the following text without pressing the ⏎Enter key.

- Type **The following list contains tips you may find both helpful and fun while you are learning about and using Windows 98. They are divided into several categories.**

Notice that as you type, the text automatically moves to the next line when it reaches the right margin defined by the 6-inch mark on the ruler. This feature of word processors is called **word wrap.**

- Press ⏎Enter twice.

After looking over the sentence, you decide to remove the word "several" from the second sentence. You can use the directional keys or the mouse to move the insertion point within the text. To move the insertion point with the mouse, position the I-beam at the location in the text where you want the insertion point to be and click the left mouse button.

The two most common means to remove text are to use the ←Backspace key to delete unwanted characters to the left of the insertion point, or the Delete key to remove the character to the right. Then you can retype the text correctly.

- Position the insertion point at the beginning of the word "several."
- Press Delete until the word and blank space are removed.
- If you see any other errors, correct them using the editing features discussed.

Formatting Text

After entering the title, you decide you want to improve its appearance by centering the title between the margins, making the characters in the title larger, and displaying the characters in a color. Enhancing the appearance of a document is called **formatting.** The Format menu contains the commands that are used to format a document, and the Format Bar contains buttons for the formatting features that are most commonly used.

Before you can apply the formatting effects, you first need to select (highlight) the text you want to format. This is the same as selecting text in a text box.

- Select the title line.
- Click ≣ Center.

Make sure the pointer is an I-beam before clicking to move the insertion point.

A selection is cleared by clicking anywhere outside the selection or by pressing a direction key.

You can also click in the left margin next to the line to select all text on the line.

The menu equivalent is Format/Paragraph/Alignment/Center.

Your screen should be similar to Figure 2-21.

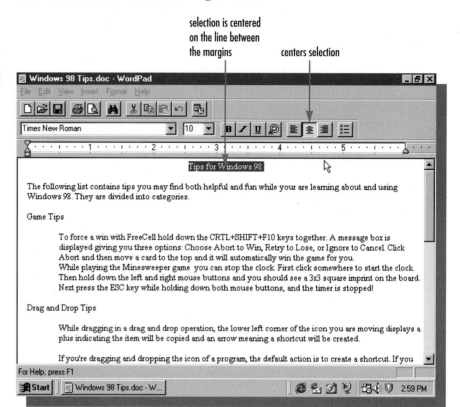

FIGURE 2-21

selection is centered
on the line between
the margins

centers selection

The selected line of text is centered between the margins. To further enhance the appearance of the title, you would like to increase the font size. **Font size** refers to the height and width of printed characters. Font size is measured in **points,** which refers to the height of the character, with a point equal to about $\frac{1}{72}$ inch. Most documents use a font size of 10 or 12 points.

The Font Size drop-down list button in the Format Bar is used to change font size. The text box shows the font size of characters in the selection is 10 points. You will increase the size to 16 points by selecting the size from the drop-down list.

The menu equivalent is Format/Font/Size.

Click ▾ to display the drop-down list.

- Open the ▾ Font Size drop-down list.
- Choose 16.

Your screen should be similar to Figure 2-22.

selected text in 16-point font size

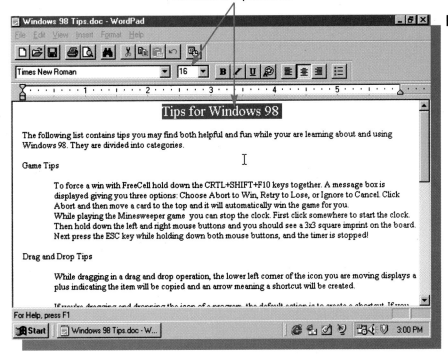

FIGURE 2-22

The text appears on the screen in 16-point font size, as it will appear when printed.

Finally, you will apply a color to the title text. The 🎨 Color button on the Format Bar can be used to change the color of the text.

- Click 🎨 Color.

- Click on a color of your choice.

- Click outside the selection to clear the highlight and see the text color.

The menu equivalent is F**o**rmat/**F**ont/ **C**olor.

Your screen should be similar to Figure 2-23.

FIGURE 2-23

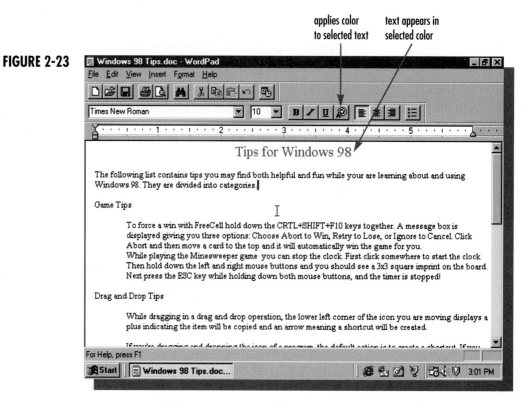

applies color to selected text

text appears in selected color

- Using the features you just learned, enter your name and the current date on the line below the title. Center the line and use a font size of 14 and a color of your choice. Add a blank line below your name.

Saving a File

Now that the text of the document is how you want it to appear, you will save the changes you have made to the document.

Concept 6: Saving Files

When you save a document you are working on, a permanent copy of your onscreen document is electronically stored as a file on a disk. While working on a document, the changes you make are stored temporarily in the computer's memory. Not until you save the document as a file on a disk are you safe from losing your work due to a power failure or other mishap.

Two commands found on the File menu of all Windows programs can be used to save a file: Save and Save As. The Save command saves a document using the same path and file name as the existing disk file, by replacing the contents of the file with the changes you made. The Save As command allows you to select a different path and/or provide a different file name. This command lets you save both an original version of a document and a revised document as two separate files.

When you save a file for the first time, either command can be used. Although many programs create automatic backup files if your work is accidentally interrupted, it is still a good idea to save your work frequently.

> The Save command shortcuts are
> Ctrl + S or 💾.

To save this file using a new file name,

- Choose File/Save As.

The Save As dialog box on your screen should be similar to Figure 2-24.

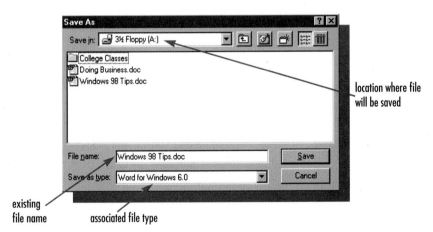

FIGURE 2-24

location where file will be saved

existing file name

associated file type

> Your dialog box may display different folders or files.

Whenever you save a file for the first time or use the Save As command, the Save As dialog box is displayed so you can specify where you want the file saved and the file name. You want to save the file to your data disk.

- If necessary, open the Save In drop-down list box to select drive A (or the drive containing your data disk) as the location to save the file.

- Enter your last name before the existing file name in the File Name text box (for example, O'Leary Windows 98 Tips).

Your computer may associate the file with another word processor or with WordPad.

The Save As Type drop-down list box displays the name of the application that will be associated with the saved file. You can change the association by selecting another file type from the drop-down list, or by including a specific file extension when naming the file to override the selection. The file extension is used by Windows to determine the application program to load when a document is opened. You will not change the default file type.

■ Click Save .

The document is saved to the disk using the specified file name. The new file name now appears in the title bar and in the taskbar button.

Previewing and Printing a Document

To see how the document will look when it is printed, you can preview it first onscreen.

The menu equivalent is File/Print Preview.

■ Click Print Preview.

Your screen should be similar to Figure 2-25.

FIGURE 2-25

entire page as it will appear when printed

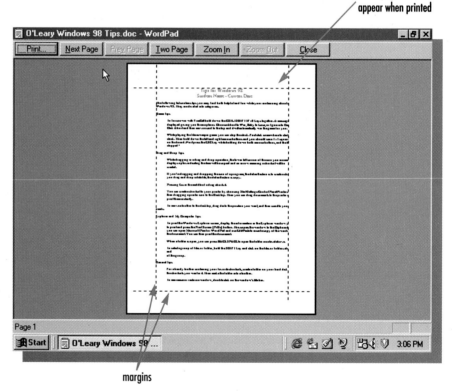

margins

Preview displays the full page as it will appear when printed. The dotted lines indicate the margin areas. The Preview window has its own set of toolbar buttons. Some are dimmed because they are not available. You like how the document looks and want to print the document.

The menu equivalent is File/Print, and the shortcuts are Ctrl+P or 🖨.

■ Click Print... .

The Print dialog box on your screen should be similar to Figure 2-26.

FIGURE 2-26

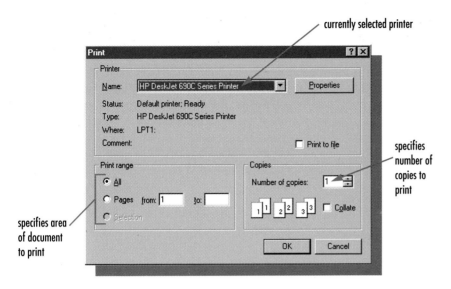

This dialog box is used to specify the printer settings. The name of the currently selected printer appears in the Printer Name text box. The Print Range area of the dialog box lets you specify how much of the document you want printed. The default setting is All. You can also select to print individual pages or text that is selected in a document. The Copies area lets you specify the number of copies.

■ If necessary, turn on the printer and make any necessary adjustment to prepare the printer to print.

■ If necessary, select the printer from the Printer Name drop-down list as specified by your instructor.

■ Click ___OK___.

The printer indicator icon 🖨 is displayed in the taskbar while printing is in progress. If you double-click on the indicator, the Printer dialog box is displayed so you can see the printer status and settings and cancel a print job if needed.

> If your printer does not print color, the title lines will appear as a shade of gray.

■ Close the WordPad window.

> File/Exit or ☒ closes the window.

Creating a Shortcut Icon

Because you will frequently be using the A drive to access files, you decide to create a shortcut icon for the drive and place it on the desktop.

Concept 7: Shortcut Icon

Shortcut icons immediately open their associated item, making them a powerful tool for increasing efficiency. You can create a shortcut icon for any programs, files, or other Windows features that you use frequently. If the shortcut is to a program, clicking the shortcut icon loads the program. If it is to a file, the shortcut loads the application associated with the file and opens the file at the same time. If it is to a feature, such as Windows Explorer, the icon shortcut displays the Exploring window. The shortcut saves you from having to select from menus or other icons in order to access the item. The shortcut icon contains a link to the appropriate application.

The menu equivalent is **File/Create Shortcut** or Create Shortcut on the My Computer shortcut menu.

A shortcut icon is different from other icons in that it displays an arrow ⬈ .

First you need to select the object for the shortcut icon.

■   Open the My Computer window.

■   Drag the A drive icon to the desktop.

■   Click [Yes] to confirm that you want to create a shortcut.

■   Close the My Computer window.

Your screen should be similar to Figure 2-27.

FIGURE 2-27

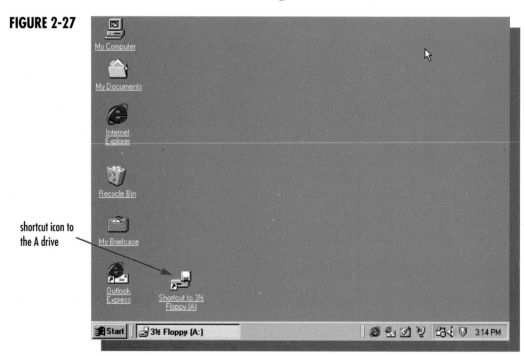

shortcut icon to the A drive

To change the default shortcut name and then to see how the shortcut works,

- Right-click on the shortcut icon and choose Rename.

- Type **A Drive**

- Press ⏎Enter.

- Click 📲 .
  A Drive

- If necessary, scroll the contents frame to display the file icon for the WordPad file you saved.

The contents of your data disk are displayed in the A Drive window. This is the same as if you had selected the A drive icon from the My Computer window. You can now see that the original file Windows 98 Tips, as well as the file you modified and saved, are both on your data disk.

Printing a Window

Sometimes it is helpful to print an image of a window you are viewing for reference. You can quickly create a copy of the active window or the entire desktop and paste it into an application program such as WordPad to print it. You will print a copy of the My Computer window you are currently viewing.

- If the My Computer window is maximized, restore it to its original size. Then size it so that it is no larger than half the width of the screen.

- Point to the file icon for the WordPad file you saved to select it.

- Press Alt + Print Screen.

- Start the WordPad program.

- Type your name on the first line of the document and the current date on the second line.

- Enter a blank line below the date.

- Click 📋 Paste.

When you use Print Screen, although it seems as if nothing happens, an image of the window is stored in Clipboard.

Pressing Print Screen alone creates a copy of the entire desktop.

Your screen should be similar to Figure 2-28.

FIGURE 2-28

window image copied into WordPad document

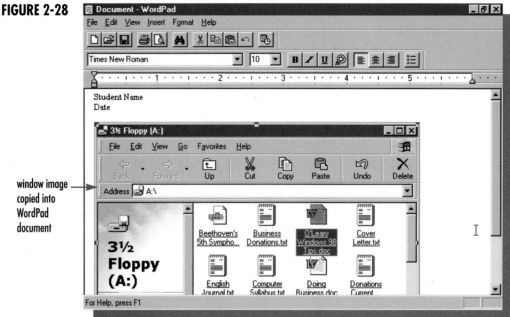

The image of the window that was copied to the Clipboard is inserted in the WordPad document.

- Preview, then print the document.
- Save the document as My Computer Window on your data disk.
- Close WordPad.
- Close the My Computer window.

Using the Recycle Bin

If you no longer need a shortcut icon, you can delete it. Unlike deleting files and folders, however, deleting the shortcut icon does not delete the original item, but only removes the shortcut you created to it. You will delete the shortcut you just created.

- Select [A Drive icon].

> You can also choose **D**elete from the object's shortcut menu or press Delete.

To delete it from the desktop, you can drag the icon to the Recycle Bin icon.

- Drag [A Drive icon] to the Recycle Bin icon.
- Click Yes to confirm the deletion.

When a folder, file, or shortcut is deleted from the hard disk, it is moved to the Recycle Bin, a special folder used to store deleted items until they are permanently removed. This protects you from accidentally deleting files or folders that you might want later. When the Recycle Bin contains files, it appears full ; otherwise it appears empty . To see the items that are in the Recycle Bin,

■ Click .

Your screen should be similar to Figure 2-29.

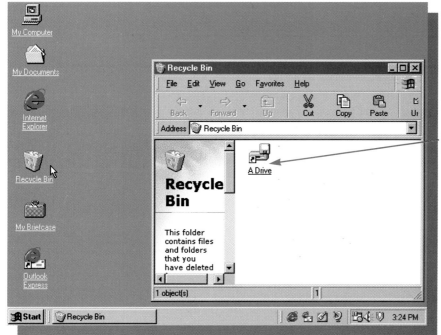

FIGURE 2-29

object stored in Recycle Bin

The Recycle Bin window is open, and a button appears in the taskbar. All files that have been deleted but not permanently removed from the hard disk are listed in the right frame of the window. You can permanently remove all or selected files from the Recycle Bin. You can also restore files from the Recycle Bin by dragging them back to the desktop, by using **F**ile/**R**estore, or by clicking Restore in the left frame to return a file to its original location.

> To remove all files, use **F**ile/Empty Recycle **B**in or click Empty Recycle Bin in the left frame.

To permanently remove the A drive shortcut,

■ Select the A drive icon.

■ Click .

> The menu equivalent is **F**ile/**D**elete, and the keyboard shortcut is Delete .

The Confirm Delete dialog box is displayed. This is another precaution against the accidental deletion of files you may want to keep.

■ Click Yes .

The A drive shortcut is removed from the list.

■ Close the Recycle Bin window.

Anything that is deleted from the hard disk appears in the Recycle Bin. The number of items the Recycle Bin can hold is determined by the size of the bin. This size is set to 10 percent of your hard disk space by default. When the bin is full, the oldest items in it are removed to make space for new items.

■ Choose Shut Down or Log Off from the Start menu as appropriate.

If you are turning the computer off, wait until the screen message is displayed indicating that it is safe to shut off your computer.

LAB REVIEW

■ ■ ■ ■ ■ ■ ■ ■ ■ ■ ■

Key Terms

active frame (WN69)	file name extension (WN74)	shortcut icon (WN96)
Clipboard (WN68)	font size (WN90)	source (WN68)
current folder (WN67)	format (disk) (WN68)	subfolder (WN65)
destination (WN68)	format (text) (WN89)	tree (WN65)
drag and drop (WN77)	hierarchy (WN65)	word processing (WN85)
edit (WN88)	main folder (WN65)	word wrap (WN89)
Explorer Bar (WN64)	path (WN67)	workspace (WN86)
extend a selection (WN79)	points (WN90)	
file name (WN74)	ruler (WN86)	

Command Summary

Command	Shortcut Key	Button	Action
Windows Explorer			
Start/**P**rograms/Windows Explorer			Starts Windows Explorer program
File/Send **T**o			Copies selected folders and/or files directly to selected location
File/**N**ew/**F**older			Creates a new folder
File/Create **S**hortcut			Creates a shortcut icon
File/**D**elete			Sends selected item to Recycle Bin or deletes it from a floppy disk
File/Rena**m**e			Changes name of selected item
Edit/**U**ndo	Ctrl + Z	Undo	Undoes the last command or action
Edit/Cu**t**	Ctrl + X	Cut	Removes selected object and copies it to Clipboard
Edit/**C**opy	Ctrl + C	Copy	Copies selected object to Clipboard

Command	Shortcut Key	Button	Action
Edit/**P**aste	Ctrl + V	Paste	Pastes object from Clipboard to new location
Edit/Select **A**ll	Ctrl + A		Selects all items in active window
View/**E**xplorer Bar/**A**ll Folders			Displays graphical representation of files and folders
Go/**U**p One Level		Up	Moves up one level in hierarchy
Tools/**F**ind/**F**iles or Folders			Locates files and folders on disks
WordPad			
⊞Start /**P**rograms/Accessories/WordPad			Starts WordPad application program
File/**O**pen	Ctrl + O		Opens an existing file
File/**S**ave	Ctrl + S		Saves a file with same name
File/Save **A**s			Saves a file with a new name
File/**P**rint	Ctrl + P		Prints document
File/Print Pre**v**iew			Displays document onscreen as it will appear when printed
File/E**x**it		✕	Closes an application
F**o**rmat/**F**ont/**S**ize		10 ▾	Changes height of characters
F**o**rmat/**F**ont/**C**olor			Changes color of characters.
F**o**rmat/**P**aragraph/**A**lignment/Center		≡	Centers selection between margins
Recycle Bin			
File/Empty Recycle **B**in			Empties Recycle Bin of all files
File/**D**elete	Delete	Delete	Deletes selected item from Recycle Bin
File/**R**estore			Returns a selected item to its original location

Matching

1. Match the following with the correct definition or function.

1) word wrap   _____   **a.** enhances the appearance of a selection

2) source   _____   **b.** changes the name of a folder or file

3) A Drive   _____   **c.** temporary storage area

4) Clipboard   _____   **d.** word processing application program

5) hierarchy   _____   **e.** the location you copy or move from

6) WordPad   _____   **f.** a shortcut icon

7) Rename   _____   **g.** graphical representation of the organization of folders on a disk

8) format   _____   **h.** moves text to the next the line when the margin setting is reached

9) ⊞   _____   **i.** chain of folders that shows the location of a file on disk

10) path   _____   **j.** indicates the folder contains subfolders

2. Use the figure below to match each action with its result.

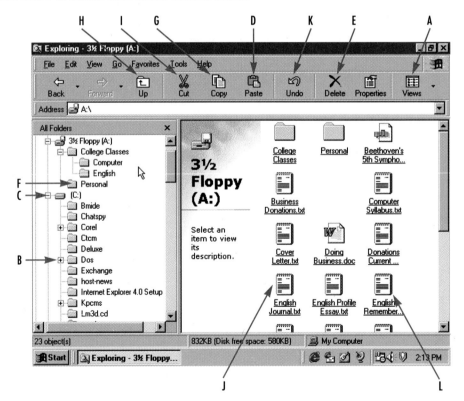

Action		Result
1) drag L	_____	**a.** opens the Personal folder
2) click D	_____	**b.** pastes Clipboard contents
3) click G	_____	**c.** removes selected item and copies it to Clipboard
4) click A	_____	**d.** collapses the folder
5) click E	_____	**e.** selects a file
6) click I	_____	**f.** changes display of icons in contents frame

Action		Result
7) click B	_____	**g.** expands the folder
8) click H	_____	**h.** copies selected item
9) click C	_____	**i.** moves up one level
10) point J	_____	**j.** deletes selected item
11) click K	_____	**k.** undoes the last action
12) click F	_____	**l.** moves or copies file

Fill-In Questions

1. In the following WordPad window, several items are identified by letters. Enter the correct term for each item in the space provided.

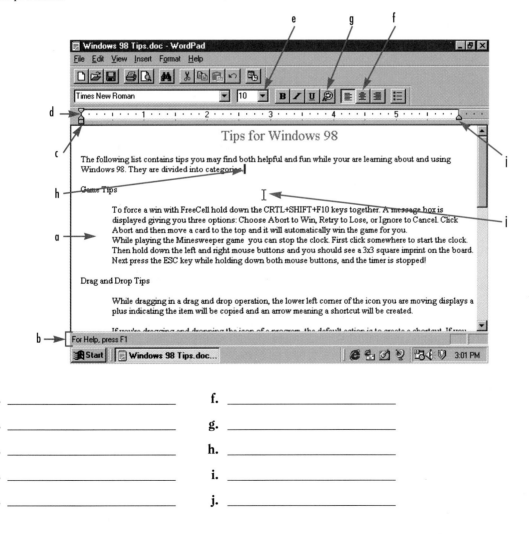

a. _____	**f.** _____
b. _____	**g.** _____
c. _____	**h.** _____
d. _____	**i.** _____
e. _____	**j.** _____

2. Complete the following statements by filling in the blanks with the correct terms.

a. The _____ drop-down list displays a brief version of the disk hierarchy.

b. To cancel the last action or command, use the _____ command.

c. _____ is used to view and organize the files on a disk.

d. All Windows applications include features that allow you to _____, _____, and _____ selections.

e. A mouse shortcut for moving and copying is to _____ a selection.

f. A(n) _____ is used to identify the contents of a file.

g. To select several files at the same time, hold down _____ while pointing to the file icons.

h. A(n) _____ or tree is a graphic representation of the organization of folders on a disk.

i. As you type using a word processor, the _____ feature automatically moves text to the next line as it reaches the right margin.

j. A temporary storage area called the _____ holds cut or copied information.

k. Clicking a(n) _____ icon opens the associated program or file.

Discussion Questions

1. You have been assigned to a research project with 12 other students, all of whom are going to share files on a file server. Describe how you plan to allocate a private folder for each student and how you plan to set up folders for the accounting, research, and cost management projects the students will be working on.

2. If you have one floppy disk drive and you want to copy a file from one floppy disk to another, how would you do it?

3. While using an application to create a file, your work is temporarily stored in the memory of your computer. The area of memory that is used to store this data is called RAM (random-access memory). Using the library or WWW as a resource, search for information about microcomputer memory and write a brief report of your findings.

4. Data compression programs are invaluable tools to create more free space for files on your disks. Windows 98 includes the data compression program DriveSpace 3 to compress both hard and floppy disks. Use Help to learn about this application. Then use the WWW to find out about how compression programs work. What are some other popular data compression programs? Write a brief report of your findings.

Hands-On Practice Exercises

Step by Step

Rating System

☆ Easy
☆☆ Moderate
☆☆☆ Difficult

1. In this problem you will expand your knowledge of Windows 98 by using Help to find out about and use the Calculator accessory.

   a. Open Help and use the Index tab to learn how to start the Calculator.

   b. Use the "Click here" shortcut in the Help window to start the Calculator application.

   c. Use the Calculator Help menu to open Calculator Help and to learn more about the Calculator application. Briefly explain the Calculator accessory features.

   d. Using Help as a guide, use the Calculator in standard and scientific views to perform the following calculations; write the answers in the spaces provided.

      1) $3 + 54 - 14 =$ _____

      2) $9321 / 22 =$ _____

      3) $753 * 23 =$ _____

      4) Average of 54, 184, 583, 831, 923 = _____

      5) Square root of 788 = _____

      6) Log of 54 = _____

   e. Return the Calculator view to Standard view.

   f. Close the Calculator window.

2. The Media Player accessory is used to play sound files or to listen to music on a CD. Your computer must have a sound card to use this program. If your system does not include speakers, check with your instructor about using a headset to listen to the sound.

   a. Open Help and use the Index tab to learn how to start the Media Player.

   b. Use the "Click here" shortcut in the Help window to start the Media Player application.

   c. Use the Media Player Help menu to learn more about the Media Player application. Briefly explain how to automatically rewind a media file.

   d. Using Help as a guide, use the Media Player to play the following files on your data disk.

     Beethoven's 5th Symphony.rmi

     The Microsoft Sound 98.wav

   e. Use Find to locate other rmi or wav files on your computer and play them with the Media Player.

   f. When you are done, close all the open windows.

3. You are working on a group project for a science class. Your group has decided to write a paper on the topic of space exploration. Each member of the group has been assigned a topic to research and write. You are responsible for coordinating the project. To make the project easier to manage, you decide to create folders for the different topics in the project to organize the documents as you receive them from the members of the group.

   a. Create a new folder named Space Project on your data disk to store the files for this project.

   b. Create three subfolders for the different sections of the project: History, Expenses, Pictures.

   c. Move the files Space Exploration Pre-1900, Space Exploration 1900–1950, and Space Exporation 1960–Present to the History folder.

   d. Move the files Moon and Shuttle to the Pictures folder.

   e. Copy the file Exploration Expenses to the Expenses folder.

   f. Delete Exploration Expenses from the main folder.

g. Rename the Expenses folder Costs.

h. Confirm that all the files have been moved or copied to the correct folders.

i. Open a new WordPad document window. Enter your name on the first line and the date on the second line. Center the lines. Increase the font to 14 points for your name and 12 points for the date. Add two blank lines below the date.

j. Switch to the Exploring Window and open the History folder.

k. Size the Exploring window to no larger than half the width of the screen. Copy an image of the window to the WordPad document.

l. Print the WordPad document.

m. Save the WordPad document as Space Exploration to the Space Project folder of your data disk.

n. Close WordPad. Close the Exploring window.

4. While doing research for a paper, you created the document Doing Business. This file should be on your data disk.

a. Start WordPad and open the Doing Business document.

b. Select all the text and increase the font size to 12 points.

c. At the top of the document, add the title "Doing Business on the Internet." Enter two blank lines below the title.

d. Increase the font size of the title to 14 points and select a color of your choice. Center the title on the line.

e. Enter your name and the current date below the last paragraph.

f. Preview and print the document.

g. Save the document using the same file name.

5. You have accepted an internship for a local charity. The charity keeps records on donations, volunteers, and donators. You would like to set up a disk to keep track of the files you create for the charity.

a. Using Windows Explorer, create two new folders on your data disk, Donations and People. Under the People folder create two subfolders, Volunteers and Donators.

b. Make the main folder active.

c. Move the file Donations Current Year to the Donations folder.

d. Copy the Volunteer file to the Volunteers subfolder.

e. Delete the Volunteer file from the main folder.

f. Copy the two files, Business Donations and Individual Donations, from the main folder to the Donators subfolder.

g. Confirm that all the files have been copied or moved to the folders.

h. Open a new WordPad document window. Enter your name on the first line and the date on the second line. Center the lines. Increase the font to 14 points for your name and 12 points for the date. Add two blank lines below the date.

i. Switch to the Exploring Window and open the Donators folder.

j. Size the Exploring window to no larger than half the width of the screen. Copy an image of the window to the WordPad document.

k. Print the WordPad document.

l. Save the WordPad document as Donators to the Donations folder of your data disk.

m. Close WordPad. Close the Exploring window.

On Your Own

6. As you learned in the lab, the Find command on the Start menu can be used to locate files on your system disk or data disk. Use Find to locate all the files on your hard disk (C:) that contain the word "window" in the name. How many were found? Search your data disk using the same word. How many were located? What is the

Containing Text text box used for? (Hint: Use the What's This? option under the Help menu.) Try out this feature by clearing the entry in the Named text box and entering the word "window" in the Containing Text box (the location to search is still your data disk). How many were found this time? Explain why different files were located. Next use the Date tab to locate all files that were modified during the last month on your hard disk. How many files did you find? Finally, locate all files containing the text "donations" on your data disk. How many files did you find? What is the Advanced tab used for? Try finding a file using this tab. When you are done, close the Find window.

7. Use Help to learn more about the Briefcase. Then answer the following questions:

a. If you want to work on files on your main computer and also on a portable computer, the Briefcase will
   _____.

b. To use Briefcase, you can _____ from shared folders on your main computer to the Briefcase icon on your portable computer.

c. When you are copying files from your main computer into Briefcase, the two computers must be connected by a _____ or _____.

d. To automatically replace the unmodified files on your main computer with the modified files in your Briefcase, you would need to _____ _____.

8. You can view the contents of the Clipboard to verify that the selection you copied is stored in it if your system has the Clipboard Viewer program installed. Clipboard Viewer is another application that is in the Accessories menu. Open and copy the My Computer window to the Clipboard. Start the Clipboard Viewer (Programs/Accessories/System Tools) to view the image of the My Computer window. Close the Clipboard Viewer.

9. Disk cleanup: Do not complete this exercise unless your instructor assigns it to you. You will not need any of the files or folders you used to complete this text. To clean up your data disk, remove all the folders from your data disk. You can now use the disk to hold other files you may need for the rest of this class.

■ ■ ■ ■ ■ ■ ■ ■ □ □ □ □

Organizing Your Work

Hierarchy

The graphic representation of the organization of folders on a disk is called a hierarchy.

File and Folder Names

When a file or folder is created, it must be assigned a file name that identifies its contents.

Concepts

Hierarchy
File and Folder Names

Copy and Move
Drag and Drop

Word Processor

Saving Files

Shortcut Icon

Copy and Move

All Windows applications include features that allow you to copy and move selected information from one location to another.

Drag and Drop

Common to all Windows applications is the ability to copy or move selections using the drag and drop feature.

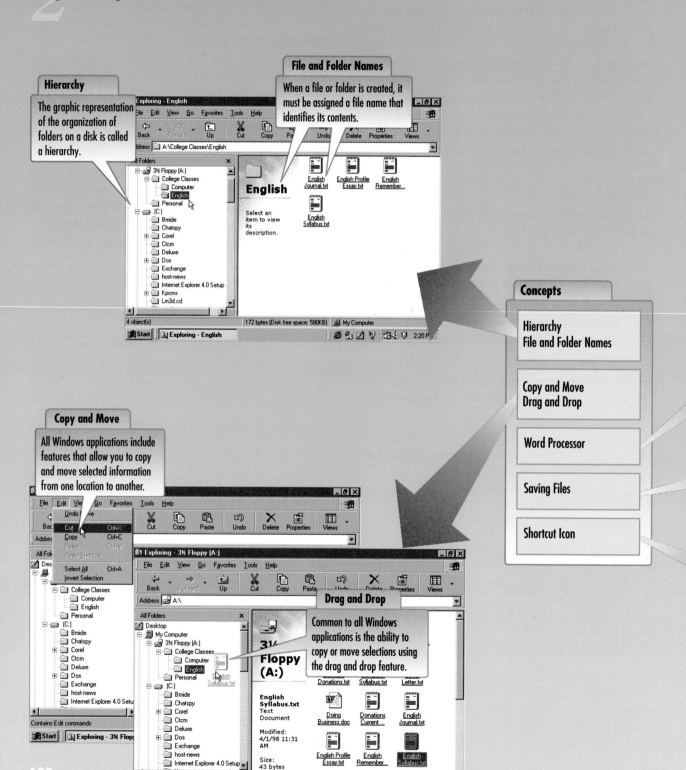

108

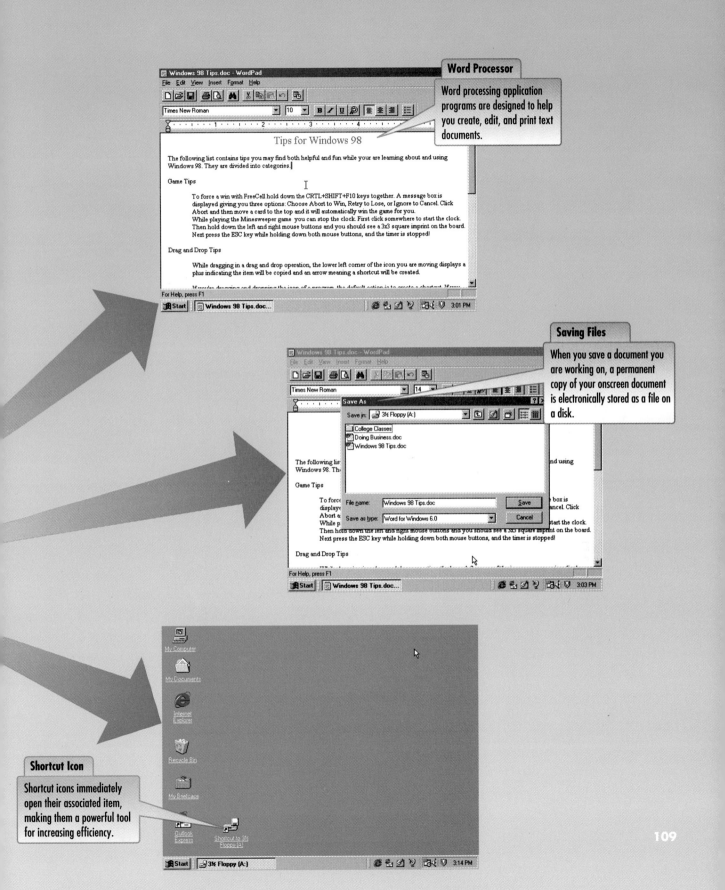

Word Processor

Word processing application programs are designed to help you create, edit, and print text documents.

Saving Files

When you save a document you are working on, a permanent copy of your onscreen document is electronically stored as a file on a disk.

Shortcut Icon

Shortcut icons immediately open their associated item, making them a powerful tool for increasing efficiency.

Appendix

Formatting a Disk

Before a new disk can be used, you must **format** or convert it from a generic state into a format that can be used by your computer. Many disks are shipped from the manufacturer in a blank (**unformatted**) form so they can be used by a variety of computers. Others are preformatted and do not need to be formatted before use.

Formatting prepares a new disk to accept information and files. Specifically, it sets up and labels the **tracks** (concentric rings where data is stored on the disk) and **sectors** (divisions of the tracks) to accept information. It checks the tracks for any bad spots that are unable to store information and marks off these areas so they cannot be used. It also sets up the area on the disk where the directory of files will be maintained.

Any disk, old or new, can be formatted. However, if you format a used disk, any files or information on it will be erased during formatting. Be careful only to format disks that do not contain information that you may want. Be especially careful when formatting that you do not accidentally format the hard disk, as all your programs and files will be erased. If you attempt to format the hard disk, Windows displays a warning message.

You will format a floppy disk. To do this, you select the drive containing the disk to be formatted and then use the Format command on the File menu.

- Place a blank floppy disk in the appropriate drive.

- Open the My Computer window.

- Select the A drive icon (or the appropriate drive for your system).

- Choose File/Format.

> Even if your disk is preformatted, you can complete the directions below and format it again.

> Do not click the disk icon, because this opens the disk, and you cannot format a disk if it is open in My Computer.

> The Format option is also on the drive shortcut menu.

Your screen should be similar to Figure A-1.

FIGURE A-1

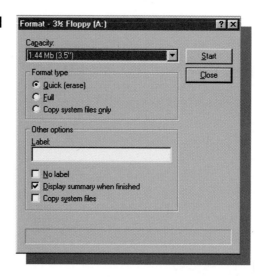

To display the drop-down list of Capacity options, click ▶ or ⊡.

The Format dialog box is displayed. Windows assumes that you want to format the disk with the maximum capacity for the drive. Not all types of floppy disks are compatible with all types of floppy-disk drives. Generally, a disk can be formatted at a capacity less than or equal to the capacity of the disk drive. For example, to format a disk at 720K in a disk drive that has a maximum capacity of 1.44MB, you would change the capacity to 720K in the capacity list box. If you are unsure of the size of the drive or disk, check with your instructor.

■   If necessary, change the capacity to the size of the disk you are formatting.

The Format Type section of the dialog box displays three options: Quick (erase), Full, and Copy System Files Only. Quick format is used only on previously formatted disks that you know are in good condition. It does not check for bad sectors on the disk. Full performs a complete format and is always used on new disks. The Copy System Files Only option will copy system files to a formatted disk without removing any existing files.

Press ⌈Tab⌉ to move to different areas of the dialog box.

■   Select Full.

The last area in the dialog box contains several additional check box options. Any number of these options can be selected. You want to include a label on the disk that will display your name. This is an electronic label that is recorded during the formatting process.

A disk label can contain up to 11 characters including spaces.

■   If necessary, clear the check mark from the No Label option.

■   Type your first initial and as much of your last name as possible in the Label text box.

You want Windows to display the summary information when formatting is done, and you do not want the system files copied to your disk.

■   If necessary, select the Display Summary When Finished option and deselect the Copy System Files option.

Your screen should be similar to Figure A-2.

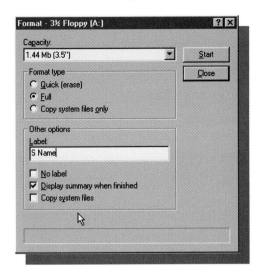

FIGURE A-2

You are now ready to format the disk in the drive specified using the settings you have selected in the dialog box.

■   Click   `Start` .

Notice the Formatting progress bar at the bottom of the dialog box. It indicates how much of the formatting task is completed. When formatting is complete, your screen should be similar to Figure A-3.

> If an informational dialog box appears indicating there is no disk in the drive, follow the directions in the box and choose Retry.

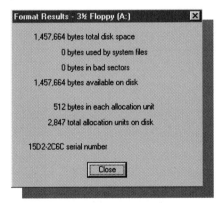

FIGURE A-3

The Format Results dialog box shows the total number of bytes on the disk and bytes available for use. If any bad sectors were located, Windows tells you the number of bytes in bad sectors. Also displayed are the number of bytes available in each allocation unit, how many allocation units were created (indicates how Windows has divided the disk for file storage into groups or sectors), and the serial number.

Click 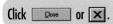 or ⊠.

If you need to format additional disks, repeat the procedure.

You have formatted your disk, and it is now ready to be used.

■   Close the Format Results dialog box.

The Format dialog box is still open, allowing you to format another disk.

■   Close the Format dialog box.

The My Computer window is active again.

■   Close the My Computer window.

Key Terms

format   WN111
sector   WN111
track   WN111
unformatted   WN111

Command Summary

Command	Action
File/Format	Formats a disk

Glossary
of Key Terms

Active content: Content from Web pages or a channel that changes on your screen, such as a stock ticker or weather map.

Active frame: Frame that contains the dotted box or highlight and will be affected by the next action you perform.

Active window: The window you can work in. It is displayed in the foreground and the title bar is a different color or intensity to distinguish it from other open windows.

Application software: Software that is designed for specific uses, such as to accomplish a task like creating a letter.

Associated file: A file that has a specific application program attached to it that will open when the file is opened.

Button: A Windows object commonly found in toolbars that initiates an action when clicked. Buttons are generally square and may contain a picture of the item they represent. When selected they appear depressed.

Capacity: The maximum number of bytes a disk can hold.

Cascade: A window arrangement that layers open windows, displaying the active window fully and only the title bars of all other open windows behind it.

Cascading menu: A menu that appears with additional options under another menu.

Channel: A Web site designed to deliver content from the Internet to your computer.

Classic style view: The standard desktop view that was used in Windows 95, the previous version of Windows.

Click: To press and release a mouse button.

Clipboard: An area of memory that temporarily stores information to be copied or moved within or between files and applications.

Cold start: Turning on the power to the computer and starting Windows 95.

Common user interface: Programs that have common features, such as menu commands and toolbars.

Current folder: The folder that is selected and will be affected by your next action.

Desktop: The opening Windows 95 screen used to display items on your screen in a similar way you might organize the work on your desk.

Destination: The location where you want to place a copy of the information stored in the Clipboard.

Dialog box: A window that requests or provides information needed to complete a command.

Double-click: To quickly press and release a mouse button twice.

Drag: To move the mouse pointer while holding down a mouse button.

Drag and drop: To copy or move a selected item by dragging it with the mouse to the new location.

Drop-down list button: A button that displays a list of additional options.

Edit: The process of correcting or changing existing text.

Explorer Bar: Displays a list of items on the left side of the window. The contents of the selected item are displayed on the right side of the window.

Extend a selection: To select more than one file at the same time.

File: A program or document stored on a disk. A disk can hold many files of different types.

File name: A name assigned to a file or a folder. It can be up to 255 characters in length.

File name extension: An extension of the file name, generally used to identify the type of file. It can be up to three characters and is separated from the file name by a period.

Folder: A named area on a disk that is used to store related subfolders and files.

Font size: The height and width of printed characters.

Format (disk): To convert a disk from its generic state into a format that can be used by your computer.

Format (text): The process of enhancing the appearance of a document.

Frame: A section of a window that can display information and scroll independently of other sections.

Graphical user interface: A design that uses graphical objects called icons, which represent the items you can select to activate the feature.

Hierarchy: The tree-like representation of the organization of folders on a disk.

Hypertext link: An object that provides a connection to another location on a disk, Web page, or folder.

Icon: A small picture that represents an object on the desktop.

Insertion point: A solid blinking vertical line that is displayed in areas where you enter text. It shows you where the next character you type will appear.

List box: A window or dialog box element that displays a list of items from which you can select.

Main folder: The top level of the hierarchy.

Maximize: To increase a window to its largest possible size.

Menu: A method used to tell a program what you want it to do. When opened it displays a list of commands from which you can select.

Menu bar: A bar that displays the menu names that can be selected.

Minimize: To decrease a window to its smallest possible size.

Mouse: A hand-held hardware device that is attached to your computer. It controls an arrow, called a pointer, that appears on your screen.

Mouse pointer: An arrow-shaped symbol that appears on your screen if you have a mouse device installed. It is used to indicate items you want to select with the mouse. The pointer may change shape depending on the task being performed.

Multitasking: The capability of the operating system to run multiple applications at the same time.

Object: An item in a window, or any set of information created in one application and inserted or stored in another application.

Operating system: A collection of programs that helps the computer manage its resources and that acts as the interface between the user and the computer.

Path: Chain of folder names that specifies the location of the folder on the disk. The drive name is always displayed at the beginning of the path. The folder names follow the drive and are separated by \.

Point: To move the mouse pointer until the tip of the pointer rests on the item you want to choose.

Points: Font size measurement, with each point about $1/72$ inch.

Program: See software.

Properties: Settings and attributes associated with an object on the screen.

Restore: To return a window to its previous size.

Ruler: Located above the document workspace in WordPad, it shows the line length in inches and the location of the margins and tabs.

Scroll arrow: Arrow in the scroll bar that moves information in the direction of the arrow, allowing new information to be displayed in the space.

Scroll bar: A window element located on the right or bottom window border that lets you display text that is not currently visible in the window. It contains scroll arrows and a scroll box.

Scroll box: A box in the scroll bar that indicates your relative position within the area of available information. The box can be moved to a general location within the area of information by dragging it up or down the scroll bar.

Scrolling menu: A menu that allows you to bring additional commands into view by using the scroll arrows at the top or bottom of the menu.

Sector: A division of a disk track.

Selection cursor: The highlight bar in a menu.

Shortcut icon: Provides quick access to the associated feature.

Shortcut menu: A menu that appears when you right-click an item. It displays common commands associated with the selected item.

Software: The step-by-step instructions that tell the computer how to do its work. Also called a program.

Source: The location that contains the information you want to cut or copy.

Status bar: A bar of information displayed at the bottom of many windows. It advises you of the status of different program conditions and features as you use the program.

Subfolder: A folder that is created under another folder.

System software: A variety of programs that coordinate the operation of the various hardware components of the computer and oversee the processing of the application programs and all input and output of the system.

Tab: A window or dialog box element that contains folder-like tabs used to access different screens of related options.

Taskbar: The bar displayed at the bottom of the desktop that contains the Start button, buttons representing active applications, the clock, and other indicators.

Task button: A button displayed in the taskbar that represents a currently open application or window.

Text box: In a dialog box, an area where you type information.

Tile: A window arrangement that resizes open windows and arranges them vertically or horizontally on the desktop.

Title bar: The top line of a window or dialog box that displays a name identifying the contents of the window or dialog box.

Toolbar: A bar of buttons commonly displayed below the menu bar. The buttons are shortcuts for many of the most common menu commands.

ToolTip: A description that is displayed when you point to a toolbar or taskbar button.

Track: One of many concentric rings where data is stored on a disk.

Tree: The hierarchical organization of folders on a disk.

Unformatted: A disk shipped from the manufacturer in a blank form so that it can be used by a variety of computers.

Warm start: Restarting the computer without turning the power switch off. This initializes the equipment for use without performing a memory check.

Web style view: The desktop or folder view that looks and operates like a Web browser program.

Window: A rectangular section on the screen that displays information and other programs.

Word processing: An application software program used to create text documents.

Word wrap: Word processing feature that wraps text to the beginning of a new line when the end of a line of text reaches the right margin.

World Wide Web (WWW): A part of the Internet that consists of information that is a graphically displayed and interconnected by hypertext links.

Workspace: The large blank area in the WordPad window where your work is displayed.

Command Summary

Command	Shortcut Key	Button	Action
Start Menu			
Programs			Opens application programs
Documents			Opens files and related programs
Settings			Changes or views computer system settings
Find			Locates folders, files, Web pages, and people
Help			Opens Windows Help program
Run			Starts a program using DOS command-line type functionality
Log off			Prepares computer to be used by somone else
Sh**u**t Down			Safely shuts down computer before power is turned off
My Computer and Explorer			
File/**N**ew/**F**older			Creates a new folder
File/F**o**rmat			Formats a disk
File/Create **S**hortcut			Creates a shortcut icon
File/**D**elete		Delete	Sends selected item to Recycle Bin or deletes it from a floppy disk
File/Rena**m**e			Changes name of a selected item
File/P**r**operties		Properties	Displays properties associated with selected object
File/Send **T**o			Copies selected folders and/or files directly to selected location

Command	Shortcut Key	Button	Action
File/**C**lose			Closes active window
Edit/**U**ndo	Ctrl + Z	Undo	Undoes last command or action
Edit/Cu**t**	Ctrl + X	Cut	Removes selected object and copies it to Clipboard
Edit/**C**opy	Ctrl + C	Copy	Copies selected object to Clipboard
Edit/**P**aste	Ctrl + V	Paste	Pastes selected object to new location
Edit/Select **A**ll	Ctrl + A		Selects all items in active window
View/**T**oolbars			Turns on/off display of selected toolbar
View/**T**oolbars/**T**ext Labels			Turns on/off display of text labels in Standard Buttons toolbar
View/**S**tatus Bar			Turns on/off display of status bar
View/**E**xplorer Bar/**A**ll Folders			Turns on/off display of the All Folders bar
View/**E**xplorer Bar/**N**one			Turns off display of Explorer Bars
View/as **W**eb Page			Switches window view between Web style and Classic style views
View/Large Ic**on**s		Views	Displays objects with large icons
View/S**m**all Icons		Views	Displays objects with small icons
View/**L**ist		Views	Displays objects in a list
View/**D**etails		Views	Displays all folder and file details
View/Arrange **I**cons/by **N**ame			Organizes icons alphabetically by name
View/Arrange **I**cons/by **T**ype			Organizes icons by type of files
View/Arrange **I**cons/by **S**i**z**e			Organizes icons by size of files
View/Arrange **I**cons/by **D**ate			Organizes icons by last modification date of files
View/Arrange **I**cons/**A**utoArrange			Automatically arranges display of icons in window as you change window size
Go/**B**ack	Alt + ←	Back	Displays previously viewed window content
Go/**F**orward	Alt + →	Forward	Displays next viewed window content after using Go/Back
Go/**U**p One Level		Up	Moves up one level in hierarchy
Tools/**F**ind/**F**iles or Folders			Locates files and folders on disk

Command	Shortcut Key	Button	Action
WordPad			
File/**O**pen	Ctrl + O		Opens an existing file
File/**S**ave	Ctrl + S		Saves a file with same name
File/Save **A**s			Saves a file with a new name
File/ **P**rint	Ctrl + P		Prints document
File/Print Pre**v**iew			Displays document onscreen as it will appear when printed
File/E**x**it			Closes an application
F**o**rmat/**F**ont/**S**ize		10	Changes height of characters
F**o**rmat/**F**ont/**C**olor			Changes color of characters
F**o**rmat/**P**aragraph/**A**lignment/Center			Centers selection between margins
Recycle Bin			
File/Empty Recycle **B**in			Empties Recycle Bin of all files
File/**D**elete	Delete	Delete	Deletes selected item from Recycle Bin
File/**R**estore			Returns a selected item to its original location

Index

Notes